Ha

Efficient XML Updates

Harald Burger

Efficient XML Updates

Index-Aware Updates for a Native XML Database System

VDM Verlag Dr. Müller

Bibliografische Information der Deutschen Nationalbibliothek:
Die Deutsche Nationalbibliothek verzeichnet diese Publikation in der Deutschen
Nationalbibliografie; detaillierte bibliografische Daten sind im Internet über
http://dnb.d-nb.de abrufbar.

Copyright © 2007 VDM Verlag Dr. Müller e. K. und Lizenzgeber
Alle Rechte vorbehalten. Saarbrücken 2007
Kontakt: info@vdm-buchverlag.de
Coverbild: www.photocase.de
Covererstellung: Marc Geber

Herstellung: Schaltungsdienst Lange o.H.G., Berlin

ISBN: 978-3-8364-0291-0

Contents

Acronyms

ACID	Atomicity Consistency Isolation Durability
API	Application Programming Interface
DBLP	Data Base systems and Logic Programming
DBMS	Data Base Management System
DIDO	Document In Document Out
DOM	Document Object Model
DTD	Document Type Definition
EBNF	Extended Backus-Naur Form
FIFO	First In First Out
GmbH	Gesellschaft mit beschränkter Haftung
GUI	Graphical User Interface
IPSI	Institut für Integrierte Publikations- und Informationssysteme
IR	Information Retrieval
JAXP	Java API for XML Processing
JDBC	Java Data Base Connectivity
NPI	Node Page Identifier
ODBC	Open Data Base Connectivity
OID	Object Identity
PDOM	Persistent DOM
PI	Processing Instruction
RDBMS	Relational Data Base Management System
SAX	Simple API for XML
SiXDML	Simple XML Data Manipulation Language
SQL	Structured Query Language
URI	Uniform Resource Identifier
URL	Uniform Resource Locator
URN	Uniform Resource Name
W3C	World Wide Web Consortium
XML	eXtensible Markup Language
XPath	XML Path Language
XPointer	XML Pointer Language
XSL	eXtensible Stylesheet Language
XSLT	eXtensible Stylesheet Language Transformations

1 Introduction

An essential feature of database management systems is the ability to insert, update, and delete data stored within them. Whereas such data manipulation in relational databases is done in a standardised, high-level, and easy-to-use manner, updates are still an area of weakness for XML databases.

Surprising little research work has been done in this field so far. For instance, updates will not be part of the impending W3C proposal for a query language for XML data sources, called XQuery [BCF+03]. So, probably for a long time to come, the way such updates are implemented will be manufacturer-dependent, if an XML database system offers them at all. Many of the XML DBMS, who do, require to retrieve a whole document, change it with an XML API like DOM or SAX, and then return it to the database – a strategy, which is called the DIDO (Document In, Document Out) approach. This can result in an insufficient performance, especially with very large documents or in data-centric contexts, where fine-grained and node-wise updates usually occur very often. For most XML database systems, including the Infonyte database system, DOM manipulation is the most common update method used.

A database management system should allow to create indices in order to provide efficient and fast access to the data. These indices represent *redundant data structures* in the database and therefore have to be kept consistent, whenever the underlying base data is manipulated. The process of keeping the indices consistent with the source by propagation of the changes is referred to as *index maintenance.* XML as an extensible data format introduces in this context the additional problem that the structure of the data can change at any time and indices are dynamic data structures, which have to adapt to the changed conditions upon updates not only on the data but also on the structure.

Updating *fragments* of an XML document with automated, transparent, and efficient index maintenance is the central theme of this thesis. The *native* XML database system Infonyte DB currently addresses the issue of fine-grained and node-wise updates with the aforementioned DIDO approach. The Simple Update API presented in this thesis aims at improving the situation by offering a way to directly manipulate XML documents in Infonyte DB (without having to do any check-out or check-in) whilst automatically and efficiently keeping the existing indices consistent with the base data.

1.1 Scope of the Thesis

In this thesis the two most prominent existing proposals for XML updates are analysed, the various methods of indexing data and structure in XML databases are investigated, and – as the main contribution – the design, implementation, and evaluation of the Simple Update application programming interface is presented, which enables fine-grained and node-wise *index-aware updates* of XML document fragments for the *native* XML database system Infonyte DB in a more abstract and more user-friendly manner than the current DOM updates in combination with the DIDO strategy mentioned above.

Index-aware updates mean, that for each update operation or sequence of update operations it is ensured, that the user-defined indices on values in the database are kept consistent with the base data. The underlying low-level mechanisms are completely hidden from the user of the API – *index maintenance* is automatically and transparently carried out in an *efficient* and *reliable* manner.

The objective of this work is not only to implement a prototypical version of the API as illustrative material and proof of concept but an outright robust and fully functional high-performance interface which can be integrated with little effort into a productive environment; therefore the *thorough and systematic testing* of the functional behaviour and also the extensive *performance evaluation* of the module are major parts of the thesis as well. These tests are automated to a high degree in order to support regression tests of future modifications and extensions of the Simple Update API (or modifications of other parts of the Infonyte database system, which might have side effects on the Simple Update API).

This study considers XML updates in *native* XML databases, specifically in Infonyte DB. Updating XML documents stored in other database systems like, for instance, relational database systems or object-oriented database systems, which are capable to handle XML data (often referred to as *XML enabled database systems*), is not the primary concern of this work, but some of the results found might be usable for such systems as well.

1.2 Organisation of the Thesis

This first chapter gives an introduction and outlines the scope of the thesis and its organisation. The second chapter elaborates on the requirements, which the Simple Update API has to fulfil. Then, in the third chapter the two most important existing proposals for XML updates are reviewed. The fourth chapter is about the indexing of data and structure in XML databases and in the fifth chapter an overview on the architecture of the Infonyte database system is given. In the sixth chapter the design and implementation of the Simple Update API is described and in the seventh chapter correctness and performance evaluation issues are considered. The eighth chapter refers to related work and chapter nine summarises and concludes.

2 Requirements

The purpose of this chapter is to describe the requirements for the Simple Update API. Note, that the keywords "must", "must not", "required", "shall", "shall not", "should", "should not", "recommended", "may", and "optional" in this chapter are to be interpreted as described in [RFC2119].

Essentially, the Simple Update API must provide the necessary functionality to modify or to delete any fragment of an XML document, or to insert new items at any position – the only restriction being, that the XML document must still be well-formed after the completion of the update operation. Schema and DTD validation is out of the scope of this thesis, the same holds for referential integrity issues and validity of intra-document or inter-document references like KEY/KEYREF and ID/IDREF identity constraints.

Apart from providing single update operations like *insert*, *replace*, and *delete*, the API must offer so-called *bulk updates*, which are sequences of single update operations to be executed logically in the given order. A *bulk update* is very similar to a *transaction*, since it also groups individual operations on the database into a sequence, which is either executed as a whole or not at all, but a bulk update provides a lower isolation level than a transaction – the concepts of transactions and isolation are explained in Subchapter 2.7 and Appendix A1.

The set of update operations should be provided in a uniform and natural way, and ambiguities in the semantics should be avoided in order to keep the Simple Update API clear and concise. The 'simple' in Simple Update API means on the one hand that only non-complex updates are covered (i.e. neither conditional updates nor FLWR updates – see Subchapter 3.1) but on the other hand also that simplicity and straightforwardness should be major considerations in the design and implementation of the API, thereby facilitating future modifications and extensions and helping to understand the inner workings of the API, too.

A list of requirements for an XML Update Language in general can be found in [Mar00] and in [Leh01].

Subsequently the requirements are outlined in detail, which the Simple Update API must or should satisfy for the individual update operations:

2.1 Insertion

The Simple Update API must provide *positional* inserts, since the order of items is an important characteristic of XML documents. Consequently, it must be possible to create and insert node-sets at a given location. These four locations should be supported as it is also formulated in [CFL+02]:

as first:

The location of the insertion is within the target node before the first child of the target node with respect to document order. After insertion, the parent node for each inserted node is the target node.

as last:

The location of the insertion is within the target node after the last child of the target node with respect to document order. After insertion, the parent node for each inserted node is the target node.

after:

The location of the insertion is directly after the target node with respect to document order. After insertion, the parent node for each inserted node is the parent of the target node.

before:

The location of the insertion is directly before the target node with respect to document order. After insertion, the parent node for each inserted node is the parent of the target node.

2.2 Replacement

It must be possible

- either to replace just the content of a node

- or to replace the node itself including all its children with a node-set; each of the nodes in this node-set can be a sub-tree with an arbitrary number of descendants

Replacing the node itself has the same effect as first inserting the replacement node-set before it and then deleting the node. This means that the target node does not retain its identity. The fact, that the same result can be accomplished by applying *replace* on the one hand and a combination of *insert* and *delete* on the other hand, admittedly is a minor contradiction to our goal of non-ambiguity, but it is often convenient to be able to express *replace* as a single, atomic operation, and therefore this trade-off is tolerated.

2.3 Deletion

The Simple Update API must provide the functionality of a deep *delete*, which stands for the deletion of a node including all its descendants.

2.4 Creation and Modification of Attributes

It must be possible

- to insert new attributes with a value into an element

- to replace the value of an existing attribute of an element

2.5 General Requirements for All Operations

After insertion, deletion and replacement, the rules for element construction apply to the parent of the inserted, deleted, or replaced node (see [BCF+03 – 3.7.1.3 Content]). Notably:

1. For each adjacent sequence of one or more atomic values, a new text node is constructed, containing the result of casting each atomic value to a string, with a single blank character inserted between adjacent values (*this issue is only relevant for insertions and replacements, not for deletions*).

2. Adjacent text nodes are coalesced into a single text node by concatenating their contents, with no intervening blanks (*this issue is also relevant for deletions*).

2.6 Index Maintenance

The consistency of indices must be guaranteed at all times, which means that on the one hand, *at no time* any other transaction (apart from the updating transaction itself) should see index entries, which refer to non-existing nodes (e.g. nodes which have not yet been added to the document), and on the other hand, if other transactions do see index entries, the correlating nodes must *always* exist (i.e. the nodes must not have been removed from the document yet). This consistency must be enforced solely by the XML database management system (i.e. needs not to be taken into account by the accessing applications), which means in our case, that the Simple Update API should take care of it and the routine of index maintenance must be entirely transparent to the users of the database system. In the event of system crashes the consistency of indices must be re-established during recovery.

2.7 Concurrency Control and Recovery

The update operations should be as fault-tolerant as possible and recovery is the key concept in providing this fault-tolerance. Since Infonyte DB is meant to be deployed as a shared database system in multi-user environments, there should be also some kind of concurrency control provided. If locking is necessary, the degree of concurrency should be as high as possible; here it is more acceptable to delay other writers than other readers.

In order to supply concurrency control the update operations should be equipped with *transactional* capabilities. A *transaction* is basically a sequence of read and write operations on the database. The definition given by Bernstein et al. in [BHG87] for a transaction is "a particular execution of a program that manipulates the database by means of Read and Write operations".

Bernstein et al. state in [BHG87] also, that the goal of concurrency control and recovery is "to ensure that transactions execute atomically, meaning that

1. each transaction accesses shared data without interfering with other transactions, and

2. if a transaction terminates normally, then all of its effects are made permanent; otherwise it has no effect at all."

This means, the so-called ACID properties (see Appendix A1) should be supported and consequently some kind of transaction management should be provided.

As will be explicated in Subchapter 6.5 on the implementation of the Simple Update API, some concessions are made on the subject of isolation due to the live behaviour of DOM, but nevertheless the updates are implemented in a transactional way as much as possible. A concept very similar to transactions are the so-called bulk-updates, which are described next.

2.8 Bulk Updates

The functionality of *bulk updates* must be provided. A *bulk update* is basically a sequence of primitive update operations, which are to be executed logically in the given order. Bulk updates are very similar to transactions, since they also group operations on the database into sequences. They are a somewhat weaker concept though, because strict enforcement of the ACID properties is not required for bulk updates. Especially with respect to the principle of isolation some compromises due to the live behaviour of DOM are made (more far-reaching than the concessions in the case of single updates), as will be more deeply explicated in Subchapters 6.4 and 6.5.

2.9 Systematic Testing and Evaluation

The Simple Update API should be as robust as possible, which means, it should be able to handle all kinds of inputs, and in case that a given combination of input is not allowed, an error should be raised or a no-op should be performed; the latter way of error handling is often standard behaviour in XML contexts – like for instance, in XSLT.

Correctness and *efficiency* are objectives, which should be achieved to a high degree. *Correctness* has to be established by thorough and systematic testing and *efficiency* has to be validated by an extensive performance evaluation.

The Simple Update API should degrade gracefully when having to deal with voluminous data or extensive sequences of update operations. Regarding the size of data the time needed for an update operation should be *logarithmic* in relation to *the total number of nodes in the database* or better and at least *linear* in relation to the *number of nodes affected by the operation*.

3 Existing Proposals for XML Updates

This chapter reviews the two most prominent proposals for a language for updating XML documents. Both of them are declarative, which means users specify *what* information they want to change in XML documents rather than *how* it should be changed procedurally. Consequently, in both languages the implementing database management system can choose an efficient strategy for the execution of the update operations, which fits its architecture best. If on the other hand users want to specify *how* to access data, they can use, for instance, a navigational interface like DOM.

3.1 Updates for XQuery

The World Wide Web Consortium (W3C for short) is currently working on a specification for a query language called XQuery with the objective to standardise the way XML data are queried. In the long run, XQuery is expected to assume a similar role in the XML world as SQL does now for the relational paradigm.

XQuery is a fully compositional and strongly typed functional language, which uses XPath expressions to select node sequences. The working draft for XQuery 1.0 [BCF+03] will probably become a recommendation in the near future. XQuery is derived from an XML query language called Quilt and borrows features and ideas from other languages like XPath, XQL, XML-QL, SQL, OQL, Lorel, and YATL. XQuery will contain XPath 2.0 as a subset.

In the underlying data model, which in turn is based on the XML Information Set [CT01] and is described in [FMM+01], an XML document is a node-labelled, directed, and acyclic graph (a *labelled tree*), in which each node has a unique identity. The basic data type for expressions in this data model is the *sequence*, which consists of distinct nodes in document order and can be empty.

There also exists a proposal for an extension of XQuery with operations for data manipulation [CFL+02], which is presented and analysed in this subchapter. This proposal is not publicly available yet, but only for preliminary review by the XML Query Working Group. In the XQuery Requirements [CFMR03] updates are referenced as follows: "Version 1.0 of the XML Query Language MUST not preclude the ability to add update capabilities in future versions."

The proposal for XQuery updates does not deal with transactional issues like atomicity and isolation (see Chapter 2 on 'Requirements'), but without any further elaboration simply assumes, that a given update works in isolation from any other update.

The syntax for updates for XQuery in EBNF notation is proposed as follows [CFL+02]:

Update	::=	SimpleUpdate | ComplexUpdate
SimpleUpdate	::=	Insert | Delete | Replace | EmptyUpdate
ComplexUpdate	::=	FLWUpdate | ConditionalUpdate

We are considering only the subset *Insert*, *Delete*, and *Replace* of the *SimpleUpdate* operations here and are not concerned with *EmptyUpdates*, since there is no use for them in our context.

Subsequently the syntax and semantics of the individual *SimpleUpdate* statements are given, as described in [CFL+02], much of it taken verbatim from this source. The syntax and semantics of each statement is clarified by a simple example:

3.1.1 The Insert Statement

Syntax:

The proposed syntax for the insert statement in EBNF notation is as follows:

Insert	::=	"insert" UpdateContent InsertLocation
InsertLocation	::=	((<"as" "last"> | <"as" "first">)? "into" TargetNode) | ("after" TargetNode) | ("before" TargetNode)
UpdateContent	::=	Expression
TargetNode	::=	Expression

Expressions are defined in the working draft for XQuery 1.0 [BCF+01]. They are based on the syntax of XPath 1.0 [CD99], which has been enhanced by additional components. What is relevant for us in this context is that *expressions* can be evaluated to determine an element node, attribute node, comment node, processing-instruction node, text node – or a sequence of these kinds of nodes.

Semantics:

The insert statement inserts a copy of the items in *UpdateContent* into the location given by *InsertLocation*. *UpdateContent* may be any sequence of items. *TargetNode* is evaluated to identify the target node, which must be a single node; if it is the empty sequence or a sequence with more than one node, an error is raised and no insertion is performed. Otherwise the insertion location is identified with respect to the target node and a copy of the update content is added at the insertion location:

into The target node may be an element or a document node; if not, an error is raised. If "as first" is specified, the insertion location is within the target node before the first child of the target node. If "as last" is specified, the insertion location is within the target node after the last child of the target node. If neither "as first" nor "as last" is specified explicitly, then "as last" is used as the default. Any attribute nodes in the update content are added as attributes of the target node, and then the rest of the update content is inserted at the insertion location. If the target node is a document node, then the update content must not contain attributes. After insertion, the parent node for each inserted node is the target node.

after The target node may be an element, comment, or processing instruction; the insertion location is directly after the target node in document order. The update content must not contain attributes. After insertion the parent node for each inserted node is the parent of the target node. If the update content contains attributes, an error is raised.

before The target node may be an element, comment, or processing instruction; the insertion location is directly before the target node in document order. The update content must not contain attributes. After insertion the parent node for each inserted node is the parent of the target node. If the update content contains attributes, an error is raised.

Example 3.1: Inserting a new element in XQuery.

The following modification statement inserts a new country before the country whose name is "Japan" in the document countries.xml. The new element is embedded in the query as a document fragment. Be aware, that in this case, there may be only one country with the name "Japan" in countries.xml, otherwise an error is raised and no operation is performed:

```
insert <country>
        <name>Jamaica</name>
        <capital>Kingston</capital>
      </country>
before document("countries.xml")//country[name='Japan']
```

3.1.2 The Delete Statement

Syntax:

The proposed syntax for the delete statement in EBNF notation is as follows:

Delete	::=	"delete" TargetNodes
TargetNodes	::=	Expression

Semantics:

The delete statement deletes all the nodes returned by *TargetNodes*. If any item returned by *TargetNodes* is not a node, an error is raised and no nodes are deleted.

Example 3.2: Deleting an element in XQuery.

The following modification statement deletes all countries whose name is "Japan" from the document countries.xml:

```
delete document("countries.xml")//country[name='Japan']
```

3.1.3 The Replace Statement

Syntax:

The proposed syntax for the replace statement in EBNF notation is as follows:

Replace	::=	"replace" <"value" "of">? TargetNode "with" UpdateContent
UpdateContent	::=	Expression
TargetNode	::=	Expression

Semantics:

The replace statement replaces the target node (returned by *TargetNode*), or the value of the target node (if "value of" is specified), with a copy of the update content returned by *Update-Content*.

TargetNode is evaluated to identify the target node, which must be a single node; if the target node is an empty sequence or a sequence with more than one node, an error is raised and no replace is performed.

The proposal states the following constraints on what can be used to replace (the value of) the *TargetNode*:

1. If *TargetNode* is an element node, *UpdateContent* must be a Content Sequence, that is any sequence of zero or more element nodes, atomic values, PI nodes, and comment nodes. This must hold regardless of whether "value of" is specified or not.

2. If *TargetNode* is an attribute node and "value of" is not specified, *UpdateContent* must be a sequence of zero or more attribute nodes. If *TargetNode* is an attribute node and "value of" is specified, *UpdateContent* must be a sequence of zero or more atomic values.

3. If *TargetNode* is a document node and "value of" is not specified, *UpdateContent* must be a document node. If *TargetNode* is a document node and "value of" is specified, *Update-Content* must be a Content Sequence.

4. If *TargetNode* is a text node, a PI node or a Comment node, and "value of" is not specified, *UpdateContent* must be a Content Sequence. If *TargetNode* is a text node, a PI node, or a Comment node, and "value of" is specified, an error is raised.

5. If *TargetNode* is a namespace node, an error is raised.

6. Whenever a Replace statement causes an atomic value to be inserted into the content of an element, the atomic value is first converted to a text node. Whenever a Replace statement causes a text node to be inserted into the content of an element, it is coalesced with adjacent text nodes.

Example 3.3: Replacing an element in XQuery.

The following update replaces the country "Japan" in the document countries.xml with the country "Jamaica". Be aware, that again there may be only one country with the name "Japan" in countries.xml, otherwise an error is raised:

```
replace document("countries.xml")//country[name='Japan'] with
    <country>
      <name>Jamaica</name>
      <capital>Kingston</capital>
    </country>
```

3.1.4 Open Issues

There are still a number of open issues in the proposal. These are the most relevant ones:

- For insertions, do attributes have to be at the beginning of the node-set in the update content if *"into"* is specified?

- How do updates relate to XML Schema validation? Is typed data still typed upon update? Is implicit validation involved? Can explicit validation be invoked on updated content?

- Can *TargetNode* be an orphan (a node without a parent); for instance, can it be a newly constructed node? As we will see, this case is allowed in the Simple Update API, because there was no obvious reason not to permit it and it might be just what the user intended. It is important to note, though, that in this case the Simple Update API must not perform any index maintenance.

- Can *TargetNode* be an empty sequence? In case yes: can/should the update operation be treated as a no-op then?

3.1.5 Discussion

Although the proposed XQuery updates are specified in a concise and precise matter for the most part, there are a number of issues with potential for improvement:

Insert "into"

In the specification of the *insert* statement the proposal misses to point out what should happen, if the update content contains attributes and there is already an attribute with the same name assigned to the element specified in *TargetNode*. It is questionable, whether the insert operation should include some replace semantics, so probably in this case an error should be raised. It is also not specified what should happen if the update content contains an attribute with the same name more than once. Probably in this case the value of the last instance of this attribute in the sequence should be used for insertion.

Insert "after" & insert "before"

Here it might be worth thinking about allowing attributes in *UpdateContent*, if the parent of *TargetNode* is an element, in order to be more consistent with the *Insert "into"* instruction – but then again the case, that an attribute with the same name is already assigned to the element, should be taken care of as well. Also, as a closer look at the proposal reveals, it is not clear, what *exactly* should happen if the *UpdateContent* contains attributes, that is, if in this case just an error should be raised and the rest of the *UpdateContent* should be inserted or if no insertion should be performed at all. The most consistent and comprehensible strategy would be, that in all cases without exception, whenever an error is raised, no update operation at all should be performed. It is also not perceivable why the *UpdateContent* should be restricted to elements, comments, or processing instructions. As we will see in Chapter 6, the Simple Update API allows text nodes in the *UpdateContent* as well, because no argument came up for not permitting them.

Delete

With regard to deletion the proposal neglects to state more precisely, that *TargetNodes* must not contain a document node, since otherwise the delete operation would result in an empty document, which is not well-formed.

Replace

The proposal fails to restrict the replacement of processing instructions or comments, if they are siblings of the document node: in these cases *UpdateContent must not* contain elements, since otherwise the operation would result in a document, which is not well-formed. The proposal should be also more restrictive on the *UpdateContent* containing attributes in order to avoid ambiguities and to prevent that the resulting document is not well-formed. Principally, it should be enforced that if the update content contains attributes, it should contain *only attributes and nothing else*, and in this case the target node *must* be an attribute, and also that *in this case only* it *may* be an attribute node; otherwise, for instance, it would be ambiguous to determine the position of the *UpdateContent* in the resulting document. Even if it is ensured that on the one hand attributes can only be replaced by attributes and on the other hand attributes can only replace other attributes, it must be specified what should happen if an attribute is replaced by another attribute, although the element already contains an attribute with the same name as the replacement attribute. The case that after the replacement operation two attributes with the same qualified name exist for the same element must certainly be avoided. Likewise, it must be specified what should happen if the update content contains an attribute with the same name more than once. Probably in this case the value of the last instance of this attribute in the sequence should be used for replacement. Since all this attribute handling makes the implementation of the replace operation rather complicated, the Simple Update API introduces a *setAttribute* operation, which takes care of the insertion and replacement of attributes (see the additional note in Subchapter 6.2.4). It is also not perceivable why, if "value of" is specified, the target node must not be a text node, a processing instruction node, or a comment node. In the Simple Update API these cases are allowed, because no argument could be found for not permitting them (except maybe that the semantics might become a bit more ambiguous since the same modification can be performed in two different ways).

3.2 XUpdate

The XML update language *XUpdate* is a proposal of the XML:DB initiative for XML databases, which consists of several smaller companies specialising in XML development. Other projects of this initiative are the XML Database API and the Simple XML Manipulation Language – SiXDML in short. The objective of these latter two projects is a general API for accessing XML databases, a kind of equivalent to the ODBC and JDBC interfaces in the realm of relational databases.

Updates in the *XUpdate* language are expressed in a descriptive way as a well-formed XML document. For the selection of the nodes, which are processed afterwards, the expression language defined by XPath is used. The *XUpdate* namespace has the following URI: http://www.xmldb.org/xupdate.

Throughout this chapter 'xu' is used as namespace prefix. In general, the style of *XUpdate* is very similar to XSLT; for instance, like in XSLT, variables can be defined and used. The design principles and requirements for *XUpdate* are given in [Mar00].

An update is expressed by an *xu:modifications* element in an XML document. An *xu:modifications* element must have a version attribute, indicating the version of *XUpdate*, which the operation requires. For the current version of *XUpdate*, the value of the version attribute should always be 1.0.

Hence an *XUpdate* document has the following layout:

```
<?xml version="1.0"?>
<xu:modifications version="1.0" xmlns:xu="http://www.xmldb.org/xupdate">
     ...
     ...
     ...
</xu:modifications>
```

The *xu:modifications* element may contain the following types of elements as children:

xu:insert-before	for the insertion of an item before another item
xu:insert-after	for the insertion of an item after another item
xu:append	for appending an item as a child of another item
xu:update	for updating the content of an item
xu:remove	for the deletion of an item
xu:rename	for renaming an item
xu:variable	for the binding of a variable to a value
xu:value-of	for obtaining the value of a variable
xu:if	for conditional updates

In the following the syntax and semantics of the individual statements in *XUpdate* are presented, as Laux and Martin describe them in [LM00]. Again, a simple example is given for each statement in order to illustrate the syntax and semantics.

3.2.1 Constructors for Document Items

XUpdate provides a number of constructors to create new document items, which subsequently can be inserted or be used as update content:

xu:element	for the creation of an element
xu:attribute	for the creation of an attribute
xu:text	for the creation of a text node
xu:processing-instruction	for the creation of a processing instruction
xu:comment	for the creation of a comment

Here is a description of the individual types of constructor elements:

Creation of elements

The *xu:element* constructor serves to create an element with a given name. It contains a mandatory *name* attribute, which specifies the name of the new element. The content of the *xu:element* element becomes the content of the new element node. The value of the *name* attribute is interpreted as an attribute value template.

Example 3.4: Creation of an element in *XUpdate*.

The following statement

```
<xu:element name="country">
  <name>Jamaica</name>
  <capital>Kingston</capital>
</xu:element>
```

creates this element:

```
<country>
  <name>Jamaica</name>
  <capital>Kingston</capital>
</country>
```

Creation of attributes

The *xu:attribute* constructor serves to add attributes to elements. It has a mandatory *name* attribute, which specifies the name of the new attribute. The content of the *xu:attribute* element becomes the string value of the new attribute node. The value of the *name* attribute is interpreted as an attribute value template.

Example 3.5: Creation of an attribute in *XUpdate*.

The following statement

```
<xu:element name="country">
  <xu:attribute name="id">25</xu:attribute>
</xu:element>
```

creates this element with an attribute:

```
<country id="25"/>
```

Creation of text

The *xu:text* element serves to create new text nodes.

Example 3.6: Creation of a text node in *XUpdate*.

The following statement

```
<xu:text>
  This is plain text
</xu:text>
```

creates this text node:

```
This is plain text
```

Creation of processing instructions

The *xu:processing-instruction* element serves to create a processing instruction node. It contains a mandatory *name* attribute, which specifies the target of the new processing instruction node. The content of the *xu:processing-instruction* element becomes the string value of the new processing instruction node. The value of the *name* attribute is interpreted as an attribute value template.

Example 3.7: Creation of a processing instruction in *XUpdate*.

The following statement

```
<xu:processing-instruction name="myapp-process">
  type="xsp"
</xu:processing-instruction>
```

creates this processing instruction:

```
<?myapp-process type="xsp"?>
```

Creation of comments

The *xu:comment* element serves to create a comment node. The content of the *xu:comment* element becomes the string value of the comment node.

Example 3.8: Creation of a comment in *XUpdate*.

The following statement

```
<xu:comment>
  This is a comment
</xu:comment>
```

creates this comment:

```
<!-- This is a comment-->
```

3.2.2 The Insert Statements

XUpdate offers two statements that support the insertion of nodes:

xu:insert-before
xu:insert-after

Syntax:

Both elements must contain a *select* attribute, which specifies the target node by an XPath expression. This expression given in the *select* attribute must evaluate to a target node set.

The content of the *xu:insert-before* or *xu:insert-after* element is the update content, which is a sequence of items with the following types: *xu:element, xu:attribute, xu:text, xu:processing-instruction,* or *xu:comment.*

Semantics:

In case of *xu:insert-before* the update content will be inserted before the target node set. In case of *xu:insert-after* the update content will be inserted after the target node set.

Example 3.9: Insertion of a new element in *XUpdate.*

The following *XUpdate* statement inserts a new country element before the country with the name "Japan":

```
<xu:modifications version="1.0" xmlns:xu="http://www.xmldb.org/xupdate">
    <xu:insert-before select="/countries/country[name='Japan']"
        <xu:element name="country">
            <name>Jamaica</name>
            <capital>Kingston</capital>
        </xu:element>
    </xu:insert-before>
</xu:modifications>
```

3.2.3 The Append Statement

Syntax:

The content of the *xu:append* element is the update content, which can be a sequence of items with the following types: *xu:element, xu:attribute, xu:text, xu:processing-instruction,* or *xu:comment.*

The *xu:append* element must contain a *select* attribute, which specifies the target node(s) as the parent(s) of the new child node(s). The expression given in the *select* attribute must evaluate to a node-set of element nodes. The optional child attribute specifies the position of the newly appended child node(s). The expression given in the *child* attribute must evaluate to an *Integer* value.

Semantics:

If the *child* attribute is omitted, the update content is appended as (a) new child node(s) of the target node(s) as the last child of the target node(s); if the *child* attribute is given, the update content is inserted as (a) new child node(s) at the given position.

Example 3.10: Appending a new element in *XUpdate*.

The following *XUpdate* statement appends a new country element as the first child of countries:

```
<xu:modifications version="1.0" xmlns:xu="http://www.xmldb.org/xupdate">
    <xu:append select="/countries" child="first()">
        <xu:element name="country">
            <name>Japan</name>
            <capital>Tokyo</capital>
        </xu:element>
    </xu:append>
</xu:modifications>
```

3.2.4 The Update Statement

Syntax:

The content of the *xu:update* element is the update content. A *xu:update* element must contain a *select* attribute, which specifies the target node(s) for the update. The expression given in the *select* attribute must evaluate to a node set.

Semantics:

The content of the target node(s) is replaced with the update content.

Example 3.11: Updating an element in *XUpdate*.

The following *XUpdate* statement updates the text content of the capital child of the country at position 11 to „Berlin":

```
<xu:modifications version="1.0" xmlns:xu="http://www.xmldb.org/xupdate">
    <xu:update select="/countries/country[11]/capital">
        Berlin
    </xu:update>
</xu:modifications>
```

3.2.5 The Remove Statement

Syntax:

The *xu:remove* element must contain a *select* attribute, which specifies the target node(s) selected by an XPath expression. The expression given in the *select* attribute must evaluate to a node set.

Semantics:

The result of this operation is the removal of the target node(s).

Example 3.12: Removing an element in *XUpdate*.

The following *XUpdate* statement removes the first occurrence of country:

```
<xu:modifications version="1.0" xmlns:xu="http://www.xmldb.org/xupdate">
    <xu:remove select="/countries/country[1]"/>
</xu:modifications>
```

3.2.6 The Rename Statement

Syntax:

The *xu:rename* element must contain a *select* attribute, which specifies the target node(s) selected by an XPath expression. The expression given in the *select* attribute must evaluate to a node-set of element or attribute nodes. An error should be raised if an attempt is made to rename any other node type.

Semantics:

With the *xu:rename* element an attribute or element node can be renamed.

Example 3.13: Renaming an element in *XUpdate*.

The following *XUpdate* statement renames the capital node of the first country to city:

```
<xu:modifications version="1.0" xmlns:xu="http://www.xmldb.org/xupdate">
    <xu:rename select="/countries/country[1]/capital">
        city
    </xu:rename>
</xu:modifications>
```

3.2.7 Variables

A variable in *XUpdate* is a name that is bound to a value. The value of the variable can be an object of any type that can be returned by expressions. *xu:variable* can be used to define a variable and assign a selected node to it. The name of the variable must be specified in the *name* attribute of the *xu:variable* element and the value of the variable must be specified in the *select* attribute of the *xu:variable* element and can be retrieved with the *xu:value-of* element. After being specified, variables carry the identifier $ as a prefix to their name.

Example 3.14: Variables in *XUpdate*.

The following *XUpdate* statement binds the object specified by the XPath expression to the variable named *capital* and uses the value of this variable to append a new country record afterwards as the last child of the *countries* element:

```
<xu:modifications version="1.0" xmlns:xu="http://www.xmldb.org/xupdate">
    <xu:variable name="capital" select="/countries/country[0]/capital"/>
    <xu:append select="/countries">
        <xu:element name="country">
            <xu:value-of select="$capital"/>
        </xu:element>
    </xu:append>
</xu:modifications>
```

3.2.8 Discussion

Generally speaking, the proposal for XUpdate is far less specific and leaves a lot more scope for interpretation than the proposed update extensions for XQuery. For instance, in the case of errors it is hardly ever specified, whether actually an error should be raised or whether it simply results in a no-operation. The XML syntax of XUpdate is furthermore far less (human) readable than the syntax used in XQuery. Also worth noting is the fact, that the currently publicly available working draft is dated 9/9/2000; therefore it is unclear, how much momentum is still behind this proposal.

As a consequence the Simple Update API is much more designed along the lines of XQuery updates than in support of XUpdate, since the updates for XQuery are far more likely to become part of a widely implemented standard in the long run.

In the following some of the omissions for the individual statements found in the proposal for XUpdate are described in detail.

Creation of attributes:

The proposal fails to point out, what should happen in case the content of the *xu:attribute* element, which becomes the string value of the new attribute node, is nested. Preferably an error should be raised, and no operation performed.

Creation of text:

A clarification is missing, what should happen in case the content of the *xu:text* element is nested. Preferably an error should be raised, and no operation performed.

Creation of processing instructions:

It is not specified, what should happen in case the content of the *xu:processing-instruction* element is nested. Preferably an error should be raised, and no operation performed.

Creation of comments:

The proposal misses to state, what should happen in case the content of the *xu:comment* element is nested. Preferably an error should be raised, and no operation performed.

The insert statements:

It is not specified, whether the content of *xu:insert-before* and *xu:insert-after* elements can be nested or not. Probably nesting should be allowed as long as the result is still a well-formed document. The proposal further fails to specify, what should happen if the content which is to be inserted contains attributes, which already exist for the parent node: Should the value of the attribute concerned be updated or should an error be raised? And: specifying *before* or *after* makes no sense with attributes, since the set of attributes belonging to an element is always unordered by definition.

The append statement:

The proposal fails to specify, what should happen if the update content contains attributes, which already exist for one of the target nodes: Should the value of the attribute concerned be updated or should an error be raised? It is also not specified, whether the update content can be nested or not. Again, nesting should probably be allowed as long as the result is still a well-formed document.

The rename statement:

The proposal neglects to specify that the content of the *xu:rename* element should be a string and nothing else.

4 Indices in XML Databases

In this chapter the two kinds of indices, which are commonly used in XML databases, are discussed and existing proposals for implementing such indices are reviewed.

Indices are special access structures offered by a database system with the objective to reduce query-processing time – a crucially important concern in most application scenarios. In fact, in a large document collection, the only way any database management system can deliver acceptable and speedy performance on the majority of queries is that the data has been indexed in some way and query processing is index based.

In other words, an *essential* requirement for query processing is to scale well to document and database size; response time should be *logarithmic in relation to the total number of nodes* in the database or better. Furthermore, indices should support range queries and sorting.

With an *effective* indexing system used for query processing, in most cases access to the base data is only necessary for delivering the end result and the necessity to traverse a document sub-tree is limited to relatively rare occasions, where the information contained in indexes is not sufficient to process the expression.

It must be stressed that indices in XML databases – as it is the case with conventional databases – represent *redundant data structures*, which have to be kept consistent, if the underlying base data is modified. This *index maintenance* upon updates is the main theme of this thesis (apart from providing the updates themselves).

Since in XML databases querying on content *and* structure is carried out as a rule, two kinds of indices are needed for efficient query processing: *indices on values* for value based selections and *indices on structure* for structural selections. In order to illustrate the need for both kinds, let's take a look at the following query:

Give me all country elements, which have a capital child element with the text value 'Kingston'.

As a path expression, this query can be expressed like this:

countries//country[capital='Kingston']

Here the predicate sub-expression "*[capital='Kingston']*" represents a value based selection, whilst the path sub-expression "*countries//country[...]*" denotes a structural selection. Value based selections can be specified on element names, attribute names, attribute values, or the text strings contained in elements, processing instructions, and comments. Structural selections are based on the structural relationships between nodes, such as ancestor-descendant, parent-child, or previous/next sibling.

For structural selections, indices on XML databases should support top-down and bottom-up traversal as a minimum, in order to cover the fundamental requirements regarding efficient information retrieval in XML documents. Ideally, all possible axes for XPath expressions should be supported by indices.

One way to distinguish between these two basic types of indices is that indices on values index *data*, whereas indices on structure index *metadata* (*data on data*).

As will be seen in the next chapter, Infonyte DB supports indices on values (cf. Subchapter 5.5.1) for collections and structure index support can be enabled individually for PDOMs (cf. Subchapter 5.5.2). The Simple Update API has to maintain only the indices on values defined for a collection, since the indices on structure are kept consistent automatically by the database management system on an update of a PDOM.

4.1 Indices on Values

Indices on values allow efficient access to atomic values of an XML document like element contents or attribute values. For this purpose they support predicates over values. An index on values consists of a combination of an element or an attribute and the values assigned to it. A special kind of an index on values is a *full-text index*, where nodes containing text are indexed by all the words in this text. Indices on values are generally well supported by extending traditional indexing schemes such as B+-trees or B*-trees.

Enhancements of full-text indices for the support of information retrieval queries:

Since XML databases are often used as an integrated framework for conventional queries *and* Information Retrieval (IR for short), there are a number of enhancements of full-text indices, which are (or should be) commonly provided by an XML database system. Especially if the DBMS is used in combination with a content management system, the support of information retrieval capabilities is an essential issue. Common practise in this context is the stemming of indices, a kind of linguistic normalisation, where the words are reduced to their root form, before they are inserted into the index. In this manner different morphological variations will match, if the text values in the query are stemmed as well before they are evaluated. Typical examples are the plural of a noun or a different tense of a verb. For English texts, Porter stemming [Por80] and Lovins stemming [Lov68] are the most commonly used. The supported search capabilities can be further enhanced by fuzzy searches in order to allow additionally to find words, which don't exactly match the searched for text. Examples are the use of thesauri for the search of synonyms or the use of ontologies for the search of generic terms. Other enhancements are proximity searches, where the maximal distance between words can be specified – with the special case of adjacency, where this distance is one, which permits it to search for phrases. In many systems used for Information Retrieval, it makes sense to offer ranked retrieval in addition to Boolean retrieval. Another commonly used technique are collations, which solve the problems in string comparison resulting from internationalisation, for instance different ordering relations in different languages and alphabets. Furthermore some DBMS provide the possibility to specify lists of unimportant and common terms (stopwords), which are not indexed in order to reduce required index space and speed up queries. The same is sometimes done with seldom-used terms, which are not likely to be queried for.

4.2 Indices on Structure

Indices on structure allow efficient evaluation of queries concerning the document structure. For this purpose they cover the structure of the database by encoding structural information like, for instance, all paths leading to each word. They should support both forward and backward navigation starting from any node. Although it is not absolutely necessary, they can be more efficiently implemented if the structure of the document is known beforehand.

In order to accelerate the processing of path expressions based on structural relationships, path based indices should support the quick identification of such relationships between nodes like, for instance, ancestor-descendant or parent-child relationships. One possibility to achieve this is the assignment of a unique ID to each individual node by a carefully chosen numbering scheme, which makes it possible to ascertain, whether, for instance, a node A is an ancestor of a node B by simply comparing the node IDs.

An interesting example in this context is the proposition of Dietz [Die82]: for two given nodes x and y of a tree, x is an ancestor of y *if and only if* x occurs before y in the pre-order traversal of T and after y in the post-order traversal. So, by traversing the tree once in pre-order and once in post-order and thereby assigning a *pre-order rank pre(v)* and a *post-order rank post(v)* to each node, ancestor-descendant relationships can be identified in constant time by comparing the pre-order and post-order ranks of the concerned nodes.

The proposition of Dietz can be expressed more formally in this way:

$$x \text{ is an ancestor of } y \quad \Leftrightarrow \quad pre(x) < pre(y) \quad \wedge \quad post(y) < post(x)$$

$$x \text{ is a descendant of } y \quad \Leftrightarrow \quad pre(y) < pre(x) \quad \wedge \quad post(x) < post(y)$$

A drawback of this approach is the fact, that in the case of insertions or deletions the pre-order and post-order ranks of many nodes may have to be recomputed, which results in a substantial overhead. The latter deficiency is somewhat alleviated in XISS [LM01], another similar example for such a numbering scheme, by using an extended pre-order and introducing a range of descendants.

Efficient indexing of paths is a major challenge for XML database systems – the main problem being here that indices on paths can become very voluminous. Features of XML, which complicate things further, are the possibilities to abbreviate paths and to narrow the result on each step by predicates, which can consist again of path expressions.

Some query engines have difficulties to evaluate ancestor/descendant relationships efficiently, so many people tend to replace // expressions by a chain of simple parent-child steps. Ideally, an expression like

/countries//capital

should be processed as fast or even faster than the equivalent expression

/countries/country/capital

A feasible approach to solve the issue of indexing paths is to create an image, which contains all existing paths in the relevant XML documents. *DataGuides* [GW97] are a good example for such a technique. A *DataGuide* is a complete and concise summary of the structure of the documents in the collection. According to Goldman and Widom in [GW99], „DataGuide construction is linear in space and time with respect to the size of the database", since the underlying data model for XML documents are trees. It is possible to generate statistics at runtime and thereby estimate the selectivity of elements and attributes. Based on this knowledge XPath queries then can be optimised. If there is a schema, it might be used for optimisation as well. DataGuides are restricted to raw paths and do not support complex path expression or regular expression queries.

Other approaches to realise indices for paths are the Index Fabric [CSF+01] and the XPath Accelerator [Gru02]. In the Index Fabric, which is conceptually similar to DataGuides, all raw paths starting from the root element are encoded as strings and then inserted into an index, which is highly optimised for string searching. The XPath Accelerator extends the aforementioned proposition of Dietz [Die82] by storing not only the pre-order and post-order rank for each node, but additionally the parent, the attribute name or the element tag, and whether the node is an attribute or an element. By exploiting this information queries using the whole family of XPath axes are supported.

5 Architecture of Infonyte DB

This chapter outlines the architecture of Infonyte DB, the *native* XML database management system, which the Simple Update API has been developed for. The Infonyte database system has evolved from research work at the Fraunhofer Institut für Integrierte Publikations- und Informationssysteme (Fraunhofer Integrated Publication and Information Systems), abbreviated as IPSI. The Infonyte GmbH, which is now in charge of the development, is a spin-off of the Fraunhofer Institut.

The main objective in the development of Infonyte DB is a scalable and modular core with little demand on main memory, which can be easily adapted to the requirements of the respective application and environment. In order to achieve this capability of easy adjustment, interaction between the XML database system and the application takes place as much as possible via standardised interfaces. The Infonyte database system is completely implemented in Java and can be used in any Java runtime environment. The database can be accessed in three ways: via the Infonyte XML Workbench (a GUI interface for administrating and querying the database), via command line utilities, and via a Java API.

Native XML databases are tailored for storing XML data by using storage structures that reflect the semistructured data model of XML. Infonyte DB uses for the storage of XML documents a persistent implementation of the Document Object Model [HHW+00, HHW+03] and thereby takes a model-mapping approach by storing an encoding of the nodes and edges of the DOM tree in secondary storage. That way every well-formed XML document can be processed.

A schema or DTD for the XML documents is not necessary, but can be optionally specified. Therefore any number of schemaless documents with arbitrary tag structures can be subsumed in a collection and subsequently any change in the structure of the documents is allowed as long as the document still is well-formed afterwards. Hereby one of the main advantages of XML, namely *extensibility* in respect to the structure of the data, is preserved. Since there is no schema or DTD required, two of the aspects of XML as *semistructured data* (see Appendix A2) are adequately supported: the structure of the data is not always known in advance and the structure may change frequently. And on the other hand, exactly this fact, that the structure of the data is not known beforehand and can change at any time, this lack of a priori knowledge about the structure, poses the main challenge for XML database systems.

Another feature worth noting is the *round-tripping* capability of Infonyte DB, which means, the original XML document can be completely reconstructed from the data stored in the PDOM document, no matter, what CDATA sections, entity usage, comments, and processing instructions it contains.

5.1 Architectural Overview

Figure 5.1 shows the architecture of the Infonyte database system. The architecture is modular; therefore the individual components can be used independently of each other with a few exceptions. The core consists of the persistent DOM (PDOM for short), on top of which the common query and transformation processors are implemented. While the latter are able to take advantage of some special features of PDOM, they can be used with other DOM implementations, too. For persistent storage it is recommended to use PDOM files, a compact native binary and proprietary format, but it's also possible to use other physical storage layers as data server like, for instance, a conventional RDBMS. Note that the XQuery interface is not implemented yet. Additional information on the architecture can be found in [Info03].

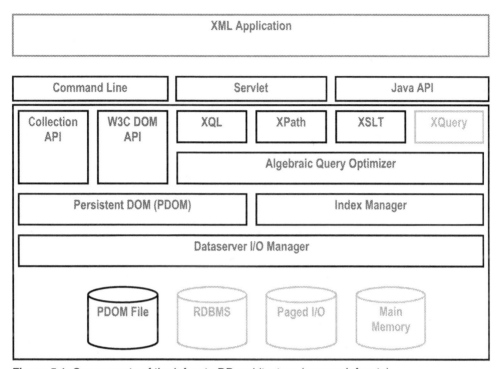

Figure 5.1: Components of the Infonyte DB architecture (source: Infonyte).

5.2 Persistent DOM

In most application scenarios, where the processing of XML documents is required, the Document Object Model [HHW+00, HHW+03] is used for the management of XML documents in main memory. This approach does not scale well for large documents, if they must be kept in main memory during the whole process, since the main memory consumption of an XML document in DOM representation is much higher than for the corresponding textual representation in secondary storage: the increase is linear in the size of the document with usually a rather large constant (five to twenty) for administrative data structures. If the limit of the available physical memory is reached or exceeded, undesirable effects like swapping or even system thrashing are likely to occur.

One possibility to address this problem of scalability is to load only the presently needed nodes into main memory. In the Persistent Document Object Model [HMF99, HMF01], on which the Infonyte database system is based, exactly that approach is taken. The central component of the model, the Persistent Object Manager, is able to swap parts of an XML document from main memory to the correlating binary file in secondary storage and back, thereby mediating between the *transient* in-memory DOM object tree and its physical representation in a *permanent* binary random access file. In its *standard* DOM API the methods for tree traversal and tree manipulation are provided as specified in the DOM Level 2 Core Specification of the W3C. On top of that, the *specific* PDOM API offers additional functionality for persistency support like commit or rollback of changes, compaction (defragmentation) of the binary files, and creation of documents, the latter functionality deliberately being left implementation specific by the W3C DOM standard. The size for the database cache can be configured in order to optimise caching according to the application scenario for efficient access to the XML data. Figure 5.2 gives an overview of the architecture:

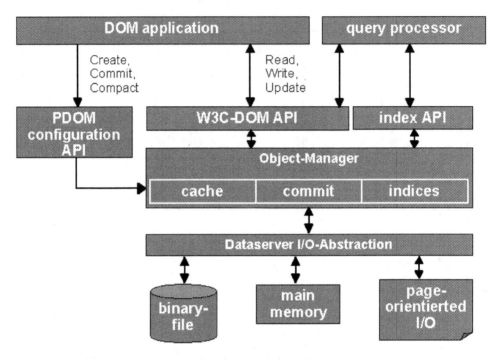

Figure 5.2: PDOM architecture overview (source: Infonyte).

The PDOM API fully implements the W3C's DOM Level 2 Core Specification. In addition, common XML standards like XPath 1.0, XQL'99, XSLT 1.0, SAX 2.0, and JAXP 1.1 for accessing and transforming XML documents are supported. On top of that, the specific PDOM API offers additional functionality like, for instance, random access to individual nodes: as we will see, each DOM node in a PDOM document has a collection wide unique node ID (in the following referred to as OID) and can be accessed by this ID by using the specific PDOM API. The node ID serves for the internal modelling of node relationships (parent-child, siblings) and can also be utilised by external applications to provide efficient access to individual nodes, for example via application internal additional index structures.

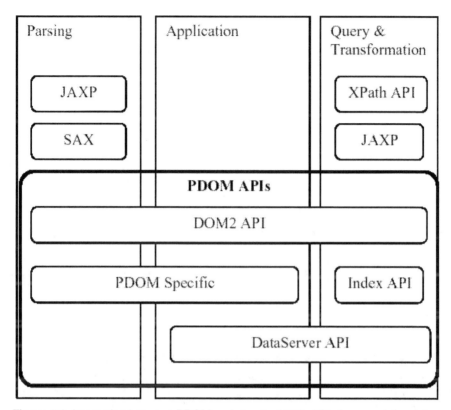

Figure 5.3: Interaction between PDOM and standard XML APIs (source: Infonyte).

The storage of the XML data is based on paged files, which means the database is efficiently partitioned into pages. Such a page is the basic transfer unit of I/O operations. In contrast to most other database systems, the size of a page is not fixed, but it can hold up to 128 objects of varying size. The data in the binary file itself is represented in a very compact way using dictionaries in order to avoid repetition of lengthy tag names and the like. On top of that, lossless(!) compression can be enabled for a PDOM document at creation time. Due to these two characteristics, the physical size of a document in the binary file can shrink down to 30 percent of the original textual size. The rationale behind this is, that the smaller the physical size of the data the less I/O has to be done. For this reason quite some implementation effort has been invested to reduce the size of data in secondary storage.

5.3 Storage of an XML Document

Each PDOM document correlates with exactly one binary file in persistent storage. This binary file consists of three different storage structures:

- a set of node pages, each containing the node data and optional structure index data of up to a maximum of 128 serialised DOM nodes

- a dictionary providing a mapping between element names e_i, attribute names a_i and more compact numeric values

- a node page index (NPI for short) that contains an array of pointers to the node pages to enable efficient node page lookups

At the head of the binary file there are two pointers, one pointing to the beginning of the NPI and one pointing to the beginning of the dictionary.

The PDOM binary file organisation is illustrated in Figure 5.4.

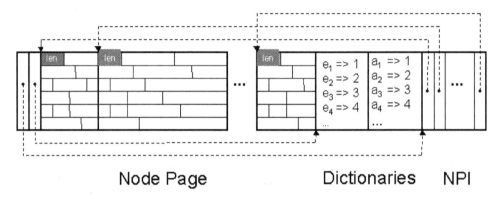

Node Page   Dictionaries   NPI

Figure 5.4: PDOM file organisation (source: Infonyte).

The internal organisation of a node page is as follows (cf. Figure 5.4):

At the beginning of the node page, the number of nodes in the page is stored (field *len*), and subsequently the nodes themselves are stored in a space efficient manner. A node page has no fixed size, since the up to 128 nodes can be of different type and size.

Each node corresponds to the aforementioned unique internal OID, which is calculated according to this formula:

$$OID = PI * 128 + I$$

PI is the number of the node page storing the node and I is the offset (in terms of number of nodes) of the node within the page. Since the OID is linked up to the physical position of the node in a specific page, it is unchangeable – unless a defragmentation (a so-called *compaction*) of the binary file takes place, in which case all OIDs are recomputed. The document element has always OID zero and in consequence is the first object in the first node page.

The format, a node is serialised into in secondary storage, can be illustrated like this:

DOM-Type | content | related objects

where

- *DOM-Type* is a type flag, which encodes the node type: element node, text node etc.

- *content* is the content of this specific type of node: for instance, PCDATA is encoded as UTF in the case of a text node; in case of an element node, the element name is encoded as a numerical value, which can be decoded via the dictionary.

- the *related objects*, if there are any, are the neighbouring nodes (i.e. children etc.) stored with their OID as reference.

If a node is deleted, it is nullified by setting its *DOM-Type* flag to an invalid type flag. Note, that thus the space formerly occupied by it (and therefore also its OID) is not reused, but constitutes dead space.

If a new node is created, it is stored in the binary file in the following way:

- if the last page found in the NPI contains less than 128 nodes, the new node is appended at the end of this page
- otherwise a new page is created and a pointer to it is added at the end of the NPI – and the new node becomes the first node in this page

If a node page is modified and written back to secondary storage, it is always completely re-serialised, appended at the end of the file, and the respective pointer in the NPI is updated.

The reason for this kind of journaling is that the modified node page might not fit in its former position anymore and appending at the end of the file is a very fast and efficient I/O operation. After such a write-back the space formerly occupied by this page constitutes a gap of dead space in the file. Such gaps can be removed by defragmentation, the aforementioned compaction, which is initiated automatically as soon as the space occupied by such gaps exceeds a given ratio of the total space used by the database system, if the system is configured accordingly.

Node pages are cached in order to provide fast access to frequently used parts of documents, whereas the almost constantly accessed NPI is *always* kept in main memory and is only written back to secondary storage in case of an explicit commit.

5.4 Collections

There are two different ways to organise data in Infonyte DB. In the first instance, a single XML document can be regarded as a database, which is represented as a PDOM document. The alternative is to subsume several PDOM documents under a *collection*, which in this case constitutes the database. A collection correlates with exactly one file directory and is implemented by a persistent dictionary containing mappings from logical document names onto XML documents, stored as PDOM documents. This persistent dictionary is stored in the collection directory. In collections the OID of each node is transformed into a collection wide unique node ID by adding to it the ID of the containing PDOM document multiplied with 2^{32}. Collections cannot be nested, so there is only one level of hierarchy.

Value indices and full-text indices (see the next Subchapter 5.5 on 'Indices') are only supported for collections and not for single PDOM documents.

5.5 Indices

Infonyte DB offers two kinds of indices: indices on values which have to be created manually by the user, and indices on structure which are automatically created and maintained by the system – unless it is configured not to support structure indices.

5.5.1 Indices on Values

As user-defined indices the Infonyte database system supports two kinds of indices on values: *data indices* and, as a special case of data indices, *full-text indices*. These indices map key values onto single nodes (single-valued) or node-sets (multi-valued) and can only be created for collections, not for single PDOM documents.

A data index definition consists of

- the *index domain*, which specifies a match pattern for the elements to be indexed (for instance, the element name and/or the namespace URI)
- a *key selector* which describes the attribute or child element whose content is used as key data
- a *data type* for the key values, e.g. *integer, long, double,* or *string*

For data indices, the supported key value types are *integer, long, double, case sensitive string,* and *lowercase string*. The nodes stored as values in the index must be elements identified by their name or wildcards like, for instance, * (and optionally their namespace). The key values can be derived from the text content of the elements, their attributes, or their descendant elements. Note that however, only the first child element, which is identified by a key selector, is considered for the index.

Value extraction for data indices is carried out in this manner: the untyped key value of a node is the XPath value as specified for "string(node)". The typed value is derived from the untyped value by applying standard Java conversion methods as, for instance

- Integer.decode(String) for *int* keys
- Long.valueOf(String) for *long* keys
- Double.valueOf(String) for *double* keys

Currently, there exists no further support for deriving the untyped key value differently or obtaining the typed value in another way.

Indices on values can be used to accelerate queries, which use the *between* operator or relational comparison operators like <, <=, =, >, and >=.

For full-text indices, the only key value type supported is *string* and the only domain supported are text nodes. The keys are derived from the text nodes by extracting the words contained in them. Before being used as keys, the individual words are converted to lowercase. Currently full-text indices index text nodes and CDATA-section nodes only, but support of indexing comments and attribute values is planned for coming versions of Infonyte DB. Word extraction uses Java java.text.BreakIterator as base. Although it can be configured for different locale settings (with their own rules what a 'word' is in terms of a locale) this essentially means that user-defined word extraction is not available.

Indices on values are implemented as persistent B*-trees. The maximal number of keys in one page is defined at creation time of the index. In case an index maps keys to node-sets, like, for instance, if the index is multi-valued, these node-sets are stored in the B*-tree with specific extensions. Similarly, the maximal number of node-set entries in one page is defined during index creation.

Each user-defined index in a collection correlates to exactly one binary file, which is stored in the collection directory.

Future enhancements:

Presently the possibilities to define indices on values are very limited in the Infonyte database system. Data indices can only index elements and can only index them by the elements' content, their child elements (no other descendants further down the line!) or their attributes. If an element is indexed by a child element and a matching element has several child elements with this name, *only the first of the child elements is considered for the index.* As already mentioned, with full-text indices only text nodes can be indexed by the words they contain.

In the next major release of Infonyte DB the possibilities of defining an index will be substantially extended. These enhanced capabilities are already taken into account in the design and implementation of the Simple Update API.

A future index definition will look similar to this:

```
<pc:index
  name = qname
  match = pattern
  use = expression
/>
```

The *name* attribute specifies the name of the index. The value of the *name* attribute is a *QName* (qualified name).

The two characteristics of the future index definitions, which are of relevance to the Simple Update API are the *match* and the *use* attributes:

- The value of the *match* attribute must be an XSLT pattern; the index applies to all nodes that match the pattern specified in the *match* attribute, which specifies the *domain* of the index.

- The *use* attribute is an expression specifying the *key* values of the index; the expression is evaluated with the node that matches the pattern of the *match* attribute as the context node. If the *use* expression returns a sequence of values, any one of these may be used for locating the node with 'pc:select(...)'. In order to make it possible to efficiently identify the indices affected by an update, *use* expressions are restricted so that they only range over descendant nodes of the indexed node.

5.5.2 Indices on Structure

Indices on structure provide for fast identification of structural relationships between nodes, such as parent-child, ancestor-descendant, or previous/next sibling. Structure index support can be disabled for a PDOM document at creation time – if it is not needed or the overhead induced by maintaining the structure index is to be avoided. If a structure index exists, the XPath and XQL processors in the Infonyte database system use it for the efficient processing of queries. Structure index information is stored with the data in the binary file correlating to a PDOM document. Note that, in contrast to the indices on values, structure indices can be defined for individual PDOM documents. Note also, that structure indices are maintained automatically after each update, so the novelty introduced by this thesis is that by updating data via the Simple Update API also the user-defined indices on values are kept consistent in the future.

If structure indices are enabled, they are implemented as a *signature tree* in the following way:

Each PDOM node page contains a set of 64-bit indices, called *signatures*, which are bit strings with this format:

$$S := < b_1, b_2, ..., b_{64} > \text{ with } b_i \in \{0, 1\}$$

Elements and attributes are hashed into such bit strings with a length of 64 bits (which is exactly the length of the LONG data type). These signatures are subdivided into an element part of 47 bits and an attribute part of 17 bits (these odd numbers were chosen, because prime numbers provide for a good hash distribution) and the hash function hashes elements and attributes into the respective parts. The signature of a parent (i.e. of an inner node) in the tree is generated out of the signatures of its immediate children by combining them bit-wise with an OR.

For the evaluation of queries first the signature of the query is ascertained likewise by applying the same hash function. If only elements are queried for, all bits in the attribute part of the signature are set to *zero* – if only attributes are queried for, the same applies to the element part. Then the comparison of signatures starts at the root. For all node signatures, which have the bit set to *one* at least in all the same positions as the searched signature, the search continues by following the references to their children. In this way the search is performed recursively down to the leaves. Since potentially a set of node signatures can match a searched signature, the search might branch off into several branches of the tree.

Note that due to the limited size of a signature the signature index can only tell if the searched element or attribute is surely not contained in the index sub-tree – if the comparison delivers a positive result, it is still possible that in fact the searched term is not contained in this sub-tree; such instances are called *false matches*. So, at the end of the described search process, a set of object signatures has been found, which point to the potentially matching objects – but only after following these references and examining the found objects it finally can be decided if they really match.

In this manner signatures make look-ahead possible and are used to efficiently exclude sub-trees, whose signature has a *zero* in any bit position, where the searched for signature has a *one*, whilst navigating in the DOM tree. This technique is called *pruning* and is utilised whenever it can speed up navigational operations like, for instance, the evaluation of patterns or XPath expressions. Signatures support both exact and partial queries.

In addition, a *document order index* is stored in the node page, which is simply the ordinal number of the node according to a pre-order traversal of the XML tree. The maintenance of the document order index can be quite expensive, if a lot of insertions are made near the beginning (in respect to pre-order) of the XML document since with such updates the ordinal number changes for the majority of the nodes.

Finally, there is also a *child order index* stored in the node page, which holds for this node what position in the ordered list of child elements it occupies. Since each child node has a reference to its parent node and each parent node an array of references to its children, previous and next siblings of a node can be efficiently found by using this index by just following the reference to the parent node and from there using the reference to the searched sibling node. The maintenance of the child order index can also be costly, in case the manipulated node has a lot of following siblings.

It is possible to defer the update of the signatures and document order index values for an individual PDOM, when the base data is modified in order to speed up the update. As soon as a commit is issued or the PDOM is accessed via XPath, the signatures and document order index values are brought up to date. The maintenance of the *child order index* can't be deferred.

In the described ways a wide range of path expressions can be processed by just using structure index information – access to the base data is only necessary for delivering the end result. On the downside, the necessary maintenance of structure indices can have a serious negative impact on the overall performance of updates, because the structure index updates are performed for every single DOM update operation. In order to circumvent this problem, structure index updates can be deferred until a sequence of update operations is committed or structure index data is explicitly accessed.

5.6 Transactional Behaviour

The Infonyte database system fully provides for atomicity and durability, but consistency and isolation are supported only to a limited extent. Collections can be opened in read-only mode, when no updates can occur and thus access is inherently safe. Matters are different if collections have been opened in read-write mode, when data manipulation is allowed; in this case concurrency control and recovery control are significant issues to be considered.

5.6.1 Concurrency Control

A major complication regarding concurrency control is the fact that changes in DOM are live, which means, changes to a node in the DOM tree are immediately reflected in all references to that node. This is in stark contrast to the usual approach in transaction management, where changes are only visible to other concurrent accessing processes after they have been explicitly committed. Hence Infonyte DB currently supports data consistency just at the DOM level; if a higher degree of synchronisation is needed, the accessing application has to take care of it.

5.6.2 Recovery Control

The Infonyte database system offers a recovery control system, which is based on a *two-phase commit protocol,* thereby *guaranteeing* atomicity and durability of updates. Changes are only made persistent if they are explicitly committed. If changes need to be undone, a PDOM document can be rolled back to the last committed state. Note, that if a PDOM document is rolled back, all transient in-memory DOM nodes based on it become invalid and therefore must not be accessed by an application anymore. After a system crash, the ensuing recovery procedure sets the database back to the last committed state, thereby ensuring the consistency of both the base data and the indices.

6 The Simple Update API

This chapter presents the Simple Update API, the design, implementation, and evaluation of which is the main contribution of this thesis. The chapter is organised as follows: first the current state of affairs regarding index maintenance in Infonyte DB is reviewed in order to clarify what kind of improvement the Simple Update API provides, then the public interface of the Simple Update API is described, next its design is explained, and afterwards the actual implementation is outlined.

6.1 The Current State of Affairs

As already mentioned in the introduction of the thesis, the current version of the Infonyte database system (version 3.1.0) supports automated index maintenance for updates only in respect to structure indices. So presently, if local changes to a document fragment are made, for instance by directly calling DOM primitives or by the XSLT extension elements for the update of nodes provided by Infonyte DB, the user-defined indices on the collections may become inconsistent. As a serious after-effect of this inconsistency the query results obtained by ensuing index lookups can be falsified – a state, which can be only be rectified then by dropping and re-creating *all* the indices (and rerunning the queries, of course).

So currently, in order to keep the indices consistent with the underlying base data, the respective XML document has to be checked out from the collection prior to an update, then the updates can be performed on the document, and afterwards the document has to be checked into the collection again.

Any deviation from this procedure can cause the aforementioned inconsistencies.

Naturally, apart from its fussiness, the present approach also causes a massive overhead on performance, since at check-out time *all* index entries for the document concerned are deleted and at check-in time *all* index entries for this document are created, which means a lot of unnecessary deletions and re-insertions of index entries. This dispensable overhead is particularly big if the updates are just made locally on small document fragments (i.e. if only a small fraction of the index entries is affected) and the document itself is large.

In the following, the Simple Update API is introduced, which renders this workaround superfluous and offers the possibility to perform fine-grained and node-wise updates, which keep the existing user-defined indices on values automatically and transparently consistent: that way these updates are *index-aware* and can be made on checked-in documents which are still in the collection – there is no need anymore to check the documents out. Only the portions of the indices are updated, which are actually affected so that the overhead for index maintenance is kept to a minimum.

Note that only user-defined indices are considered and have to be updated by the Simple Update API, since the maintenance of structure indices is already done automatically by the database system.

The API is designed to support the planned extended possibilities of indexing a collection in the next major release of Infonyte DB (see Subchapter 5.5.1).

6.2 The Public Interface

As already mentioned above, the Simple Update API is designed along the lines of the proposed updates for XQuery [CFL+02]. Its public interface consists of the following five methods:

insert	for the positional insertion of new items
delete	for the deletion of existing items
replace	for the replacement of existing items or the replacement of content
setAttribute	for the insertion of new attributes or the replacement of the value of existing attributes
doBulkUpdate	for the execution of a sequence of update operations

Furthermore the API contains the public class *BulkUpdateList,* which can be used to combine
a sequence of update operations to an atomic transaction.

General note about the restrictions on the parameters of the methods:

If in doubt, whether to allow a constellation of parameter values or not, in most cases the
decision was made in favour of not allowing it. The deciding factor was this: since the Infonyte database system is already in use in many production environments, it could be very
painful for the users, if any part of the Infonyte API becomes more restrictive from one version to the next, which would be the case if it should be realised later on that a particular
constellation is not feasible and should not be allowed anymore. In such a case a lot of adjustment might be necessary to get existing applications working with the updated version of
Infonyte DB. The other way round, relaxing any restrictions in future versions of the API, if it
turns out later on that there is no problem allowing a formerly forbidden constellation, poses
no problem in this respect.

Subsequently the individual public high-level methods are presented in detail:

6.2.1 The Method Insert

The method declaration of *insert* is as follows:

```
insert(Node targetNode, String location, Object updateContent)
```

Parameters:

- *targetNode*   is used as the target node for the insert operation
- *location*   is the location, where the new node or node-set will be inserted
- *updateContent*   is the content to be inserted and can be a single node or a node-set

Effect:

The new nodes in *updateContent* are inserted at the given position depending on the value
specified in the parameter *location*. If the parameter *location* is omitted, its default is "as-last"
– if given, its value must be one of the following:

"as-first"	the new nodes in *updateContent* are inserted before the first child of the target node.
"as-last"	the new nodes in *updateContent* are inserted after the last child of the target node.

"before"   the new nodes in *updateContent* are inserted as siblings before the target node.

"after"   the new nodes in *updateContent* are inserted as siblings after the target node

Restrictions on the parameters:

In the following cases, the operation fails, no insertion is performed, and an appropriate exception is thrown:

- The target node or one of the new nodes in *updateContent* is null.
- One of the new nodes in *updateContent* has a parent. The Simple Update API does not support any *move* semantics directly in order to keep the semantics clean. A *move* operation must be carried out explicitly by a deletion and subsequent insertion.
- The parameter *location* is given and has any other value than "as-first", "as-last", "before", or "after".
- The target node or one of the new nodes in *updateContent* is an attribute node. New attribute nodes can only be inserted with *setAttribute* (see below).
- The location is "as-first" or "as-last" and the target node is not an element.
- The location is "before" or "after", the target node is the document element or a sibling of the document element (in DOM semantics: the parent of the target node is the document element) and one of the new nodes is not a comment node or a PI node – otherwise the document would not be well-formed afterwards.

6.2.2 The Method Replace

The method declaration of *replace* is as follows:

```
replace(Node targetNode, Object updateContent, boolean valueOf)
```

Parameters:

- *targetNode*   is used as the target node for the replace operation
- *updateContent*   is the replacement value or the replacement node-set (can be a single node or a node-set)
- *valueOf*   if true, the content of the node is replaced
      if false, the node itself is replaced

Case 1: Replacing the content of a node (*valueOf* is set to true)

Effect:

If the value of the parameter *valueOf* is true, the string given in *updateContent* replaces the text content of the target node.

Restrictions on the parameters:

In the following cases, the operation fails, no update is performed, and an appropriate exception is thrown:

- The data type of at least one item in *updateContent* is not 'String'.
- The target node or *updateContent* is null. If *updateContent* were null, the effect would be equivalent to deleting the node, which has to be done with the delete operation.
- *updateContent* is the empty string. According to [HHW+00], a document in normal form does not contain empty text nodes in DOM Level 2 and in the W3C working draft *'XQuery 1.0 and XPath 2.0 Data Model'* [FMM+01] it is explicitly stated that "text nodes must sat-

isfy the following constraint: A text node must not contain the empty string as its content". So again, the effect would be equivalent to deleting the node, which has to be done with the *delete* operation, as already stated.

Note, that there is a difference in Java between a null string and the empty string.

- The target node is not a text node, a comment node, a PI node, or a CDATA section node. The target node must not be an attribute, because the content of an attribute has to be replaced with *setAttribute*. The target node must not be an element, since elements can have several text nodes as children, so it would be ambiguous to decide which one of them to replace.

Case 2: Replacing a node (*valueOf* is set to false)

Effect:

If the value of the parameter *valueOf* is false, the node or the node-set in *updateContent* replaces the target node including its children.

Restrictions on the parameters:

In the following cases, the operation fails, no update is performed, and an appropriate exception is thrown:

- The data type of at least one of the replacement nodes in *updateContent* is not 'Node'.
- The target node or one of the replacement nodes in *updateContent* is null.
- One of the replacement nodes in *updateContent* has a parent. The Simple Update API does not support any *move* semantics directly in order to keep the semantics clean. A *move* operation must be carried out explicitly by a deletion and subsequent insertion.
- The target node is the document element. This is in contrast to the XQuery updates [CFL+02], where replacing the document element is allowed (see Subchapter 3.1.3). Since for the Simple Update API the operation of replacing a node is equivalent to an insertion followed by a deletion, this would temporarily result in two document elements in the same document. And furthermore, the deletion of a document element is also not allowed.
- The target node is a sibling of the document element node and the replacement node is not a comment node or a PI node – otherwise the resulting document would not be well-formed.
- The target node or at least one of the replacement nodes is an attribute node. The replacement of an attribute by another attribute can only be done by deleting the old one with *delete*, and inserting the new one with *setAttribute* (see below).

6.2.3 The Method Delete

The method declaration of *delete* is as follows:

```
delete(Node targetNode)
```

Parameters:

- *targetNode*   is used as the target node for the delete operation

Effect:

The target node including its children (deep delete) will be deleted.

Restrictions on the parameters:

In the following cases, the update fails, no deletion is performed, and an appropriate exception is thrown:

- The target node is null.
- The target node is the document element node – otherwise the resulting document would not contain any elements at all afterwards and thus it would not be well-formed anymore.

6.2.4 The Method SetAttribute

The method declaration of *setAttribute* is as follows:

```
setAttribute(Node targetNode, String attributeName, String attributeValue)
```

Parameters:

- *targetNode*   is used as the target node for the operation
- *attributeValue*   contains the attribute value
- *attributeName*   contains the attribute name

Effect:

If the attribute *attributeName* of the target node already exists, the value given in *attributeValue* will be assigned to it, thereby replacing the old value. If the attribute *attributeName* of the target node does not yet exist, a new attribute *attributeName* with the value given in *attributeValue* will be created. The attribute name is mandatory and supplies the (qualified) name of the attribute. If this name contains a prefix it must be resolvable from the namespace declarations in scope of the affected element. The attribute value can be null or the empty string, in which case the value of the attribute will be the empty string.

Restrictions on the parameters:

In the following cases, the update fails, no operation is performed, and an appropriate exception is thrown:

- The target node is null.
- The attribute name is null or the empty string.
- The target node is not an element.

Additional note:

There are a number of reasons, why the *setAttribute* method is introduced, even though it has no equivalent in the proposed simple updates for XQuery [CFL+02]. The first reason is that the *insert* method is not very well suited for the insertion of new attributes, since the *insert* method *always* provides for positional insertion – and it is not possible to insert an attribute at a specified position. The second reason is that in XSLT (which is a platform also to be supported by the Simple Update API), it is not possible to create a stand-alone attribute – so without a *setAttribute* method, it would be necessary in XSLT to create a dummy element in order to accommodate the attributes one intends to insert. Additionally, the reasons, why it might be infeasible to carry out the replacement of existing attributes with the *replace* method, have already been given in the discussion of the proposed update extension for XQuery (see Subchapter 3.1.5).

6.2.5 The Method DoBulkUpdate

The method declaration of doBulkUpdate is as follows:

```
doBulkUpdate(BulkUpdateList updateList)
```

Parameters:

- *updateList* contains the sequence of update operations

Effect:

The sequence of update operations given in *updateList* is executed. A *commit* is issued only if all operations have been executed successfully otherwise a *rollback* is done.

Restrictions on the parameters:

In the following cases, the update fails, no operation is performed, and an appropriate exception is thrown:

- The *updateList* is null.

6.3 Architectural Design

The architecture of the Simple Update API is subdivided in 3 layers in order to avoid implementing the same functionality repeatedly in different parts of the source code. Subsequently each layer is described in detail:

6.3.1 Top Layer

The top layer consists of the already introduced *public* methods *insert*, *delete*, *replace*, *setAttribute*, and *doBulkUpdate*.

The outward behaviour of these methods has already been presented in Subchapter 6.2 – the internal modus operandi of the methods in the top-level layer is as follows:

1. It is first checked, if all the parameters of the subsequent calls are allowed as they are given (by calling the respective methods – see Subchapter 6.5.1). Note, that if node-sets are used for replacements or insertions *all* nodes in the node-set are inspected. With bulk updates first *all* parameters *for the whole sequence* of update operations are checked. If an illegal constellation of parameters is found, the operation is cancelled, no update is performed at all, and an error is raised (that is to say an appropriate exception is thrown).

2. The respective medium-level and low-level methods are called; in case of a bulk update the calls are made for the whole sequence of update operations.

3. After the successful completion of the update operation(s) a commit is issued – in case an error occurred a rollback is performed.

6.3.2 Middle Layer

Considering that by the *insert* operation a whole node-set can be inserted and by the *replace* operation a node can be replaced with a whole node-set, an additional middle layer is needed for these two operations in order to allow the insertion of whole node-sets and the usage of whole node-sets as a replacement when replacing a node since the low-level methods operate on single nodes only. There is no need for a medium layer for the *setAttribute* and *delete* operations, since these operations are always performed on single nodes and with single nodes.

Thus the middle layer comprises these *private* methods:

insertMediumLevel   for the positional insertion of a node-set or a single node

replaceMediumLevel   for the replacement of a single node with a single node or a node-set – or for the replacement of the content of a single node

insertMediumLevel accepts both a node-set and a single node as the *update content*, which is to be inserted. In case the *update content* is a single node, the call is just passed through to *insertLowLevel*. If on the other hand the update content is a node-set, *insertMediumLevel* inserts the first node in the *update content* at the desired location and then inserts all the other nodes contained in the *update content* right after it in FIFO order, in each case by calling *insertLowLevel*.

replaceMediumLevel, if called with the parameter *valueOf* set to false, accepts both a node-set and a single node as the *update content*, which is to be used as a replacement. In case the *update content* is a single node, the call is just passed through to *replaceLowLevel*. If the update content is a node-set, *replaceLowLevel* replaces the *target node* with the first node in the node-set in the *update content* by calling *replaceLowLevel* and then inserts all the other nodes contained in the *update content* right after it, again in FIFO order, by calling *insertLowLevel* for each node. If *replaceMediumLevel* is called with the parameter *valueOf* set to true, the call is always just passed through to *replaceLowLevel.*

6.3.3 Bottom Layer

At the bottom layer are the *private* methods, which operate on a single node:

insertLowLevel   for the positional insertion *of a single node*

deleteLowLevel   for the deletion *of a single node*

replaceLowLevel   for the replacement of a single node *with a single node* or the replacement of the content of *a single node*

setAttributeLowLevel   for the insertion of new attributes into a *single node* or the replacement of the value of existing attributes of a *single node*

The general strategy, which these methods implement, is described in Subchapter 6.4.4 and the detailed algorithm is explained in Subchapter 6.5.6.

6.3.4 Correlation Between the Layers

Figure 6.1 illustrates the correlation between the methods in the different layers. In case a node-set is inserted or used as a replacement, *insertMediumLevel* respectively *replaceMediumLevel* calls *insertLowLevel* repeatedly:

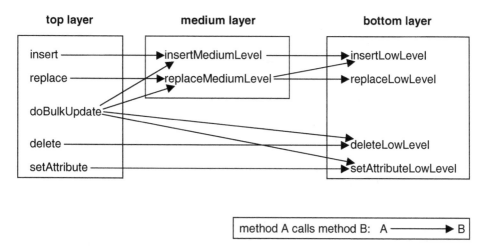

Figure 6.1: Calling relations between the methods.

6.4 Index Maintenance

Basically, there are two approaches to index maintenance: *incremental maintenance* and the brute-force approach, rebuilding *all* the indices from scratch.

The focus in this thesis is on *incremental index maintenance*, since reconstructing the indices from scratch after each update would be only more efficient in the case of massive changes to the database. In general the cost of an update should be *proportional to the size of the update* and not *proportional to the size of the database* (as it is the case with the naive approach of recomputing the indices with each update). Evaluating, when this *complete reconstruction* is the more favourable option nevertheless and acting accordingly is beyond the scope of this thesis, even if a complete rebuilding in rare cases might yield a better performance. Some empirical evidence can be gathered from Chapter 7 on testing and evaluation, though.

For index maintenance only deletions and insertions need to be considered, since a replacement of index entries is nothing else than an insertion followed by a deletion.

After each of the update operations, all adjacent text nodes, which may have been produced by the update operation, are merged into a single text node. This procedure, which makes sure that the rules for element construction (see Subchapter 2.5) are enforced, is also called *normalisation*. The important aspect is here, that if such a merging of text nodes is necessary, index maintenance has to be taken care of again, which is achieved by simply calling the *replace [content]* and *delete* methods accordingly, since this merging of text nodes is realised as the replacement of the content of one of these text nodes with the concatenated content of the text nodes to merge and the subsequent deletion of the other text nodes.

6.4.1 Prerequisite and Definitions

The technique used for index maintenance is basically identical for all update operations and is outlined in the next subchapter after a necessary prerequisite, some preparing definitions and a short description of the used variables are given.

Prerequisite:

An *indispensable* precondition for the correct functioning of the algorithm for index mainte-nance is the restriction that the key-expressions of indices only range over the descendants of indexed nodes.

In order to facilitate the description of the algorithm for the index maintenance some defini-tions of node-sets and sets of index entries are given, which are used later on:

Definition 1: context nodes of an update

The *context nodes* of an update are all nodes which remain in the document, but whose content may change due to an update. Consequently, if they are indexed, their key-value(s) may change during an update and the indices need to be updated accordingly. Due to the aforementioned prerequisite, the context nodes are limited to all ancestors of the target node and depending on the specific operation the target node itself is also included or not.

Definition 2: context entries of an index

The entries in an index correlating to the matching context nodes of an update are the *con-text entries* of this index.

Definition 3: sub-tree nodes

The set comprising a node and all descendants of this node are the *sub-tree nodes*.

Definition 4: sub-tree entries of an index

The entries in an index correlating to a matching node and all its matching descendants are the *sub-tree entries* of this index.

There are two more node-sets, which are of relevance:

- The *set of deleted nodes* consists of the target node in a delete or replace operation *and* all its descendants. If they are indexed, their correlating index entries need to be removed from the index.

- The *set of inserted nodes* is the node-set inserted by a replace or insert operation.

In order to make the understanding of the algorithm easier, a short description of the vari-ables used in the algorithm is given:

contextEntriesBeforeUpdate[i]:	an array of (key, node ID list) tuples, where for each key value occurring in any context node (relating to the before-update state) a *list* of the node IDs of the matching context nodes for index i is stored.
contextEntriesAfterUpdate[i]:	same as *contextEntriesBeforeUpdate[i]* but relating to the after-update state of the context.
oldSubtreeEntries[i]:	an array of (key, node ID list) tuples, where for each key value occurring in the target node (which is to be removed by the update) or any of its descendants, a *list* of the node IDs of the matching sub-tree nodes for index i is stored.
newSubtreeEntries[i]:	same as *oldSubtreeEntries[i]* but relating to the sub-tree of the node, which is to be inserted by the update.

6.4.2 Basic Layout of the Algorithm for Index Maintenance

Listing 6.1 gives the basic layout of the algorithm for index maintenance (in a way the core of this thesis) by describing the calculation and processing of the relevant sets of index entries in pseudo-code (refer to Subchapter 6.4.4 for information on the degree of locking during each step):

```
begin
(1) for each existing index i

        (1.1) compute the set of context entries before the update

        (1.2) store the set computed in step (1.1) in contextEntriesBeforeUpdate[i]

        (1.3) if the target node will be removed
                (1.3.1) compute the set of index entries for the target node and all its
                        descendants
                (1.3.2) store the set computed in step (1.3.1) in oldSubtreeEntries[i]
                end if

    end for

(2) perform the DOM update

(3) for each existing index i

        (3.1) compute the context entries after the update

        (3.2) store the set computed in step (3.1) in contextEntriesAfterUpdate[i]

        (3.3) compute the delta in context entries and update the index i accordingly:
                (3.3.1) compute the set of index entries after the update, which were not
                        contained in the set of context entries before the update, namely:
                        contextEntriesAfterUpdate[i] – contextEntriesBeforeUpdate[i]
                (3.3.2) insert the set computed in step (3.3.1) into index i
                (3.3.3) compute the set of index entries, which were contained in the
                        set of context entries before the update but are not anymore in the
                        set of context entries after the update, namely:
                        contextEntriesBeforeUpdate[i] – contextEntriesAfterUpdate[i]
                (3.3.4) remove the set computed in step (3.3.3) from index i

        (3.4) if a node has been inserted
                (3.4.1) compute the set of index entries for the inserted node and for all its
                        descendants
                (3.4.2) store the set computed in step (3.4.1) in newSubtreeEntries[i]
                end if

        (3.5) insert the set newSubtreeEntries[i] into index i

        (3.6) remove the set oldSubtreeEntries[i] from index i

    end for
end
```

Listing 6.1: Basic layout of the algorithm for index maintenance.

6.4.3 Calculation of the Delta in Index Entries

An important measure for keeping the overhead for index maintenance as low as possible is first to determine if an index is affected by an update operation at all and in case it is, to find out which of its entries are actually involved and *only* act on these index entries. The algorithm is a kind of differential algorithm, which translates the delta in the DOM tree caused by the update into a delta in index entries for each index and accordingly inserts entries into the respective index or removes entries from the respective index.

After step (3.2) (cf. Listing 6.1) the delta, which the update induces on index i can be determined. The following sets of index entries are significant for the calculation of this delta:

- the difference between sets
  $$REMOVE_i = contextEntriesBeforeUpdate[i] - contextEntriesAfterUpdate[i]$$
  These are all index entries, which are contained in contextEntriesBeforeUpdate[i] *but not* in contextEntriesAfterUpdate[i]. These index entries have been made obsolete by the update and therefore have to be removed from index i.

- the difference between sets
  $$ADD_i = contextEntriesAfterUpdate[i] - contextEntriesBeforeUpdate[i]$$
  These are all index entries, which are contained in contextEntriesAfterUpdate[i] *but not* in contextEntriesBeforeUpdate[i]. These index entries have been created by the update and therefore have to be added to index i.

- *the intersection of sets*
  $$KEEP_i = contextEntriesBeforeUpdate[i] \cap contextEntriesAfterUpdate[i]$$
  These are all index entries, which are contained in contextEntriesBeforeUpdate[i] *and also* in contextEntriesAfterUpdate[i]. These index entries are not affected by the update, and therefore no action regarding index i needs to be taken for them.

- oldSubtreeEntries[i]: all index entries in this set have been made obsolete by the update and therefore have to be removed from index i since the corresponding nodes have been removed from the DOM tree by the update.

- newSubtreeEntries[i]: all index entries in this set have to be added to index i since the corresponding nodes have been added to the DOM tree by the update.

By removing only the index entries in $REMOVE_i \cup oldSubtreeEntries[i]$ and adding only the index entries in $ADD_i \cup newSubtreeEntries[i]$, the updates on index i are kept to the bare minimum and therefore the induced (and expensive) I/O, when subsequently the dirty index pages are written back to secondary storage, is as low as possible.

In contrast, a naive but functioning approach would have been to remove first *all* index entries in *contextEntriesBeforeUpdate[i]* $\cup$ *oldSubtreeEntries[i]* before the DOM update and then to add *all* index entries in *contextEntriesAfterUpdate[i]* $\cup$ *newSubtreeEntries[i]* after the DOM update. This would have caused unnecessary deletions and re-insertions on the index in regard to the context entries and the avoidable access to secondary storage resulting from these superfluous operations can be quite extensive and therefore expensive – especially if $KEEP_i$ is a large set.

If $REMOVE_i \cup oldSubtreeEntries[i] \cup ADD_i \cup newSubtreeEntries[i]$ is the empty set, then the update is not relevant for index i and maintenance of index i is not necessary.

As we will see later when the algorithm is presented in detail, the obsolete index entries are not removed at once, but in order to maximise the degree of concurrency are initially just marked as *phantom entries*, and are only removed later in a *non-critical section*, where there is no locking necessary anymore and no other accessing processes are blocked. *Phantom entries* are still physically present in the index but are ignored for index lookups. In the following high-level presentation of the algorithm the process of marking and deleting phantom entries is explicitly stated and the degree of locking is pointed out for each step.

6.4.4 General Strategy in High-Level Notation

For all the bottom layer methods, namely *insertLowLevel*, *deleteLowLevel*, *replaceLowLevel*, and *setAttributeLowLevel*, the general strategy is the same. They all perform these three basic steps:

step 1:

- compute the *context entries before the update* for all indices
- compute the old sub-tree entries, which are to be deleted, for all indices
- *locking:* no locking necessary in step 1, since no changes on data or indices are made

step 2:

- perform the update on the PDOM
- compute the *context entries after the update* for all indices
- compute the new sub-tree entries, which are to be inserted, for all indices
- insert all the new entries (context and sub-tree) into the indices
- convert the entries (context and sub-tree), which are to be deleted, into phantom entries
- mark the PDOM and the indices as dirty
- *locking:* during the whole duration of step 2, all readers and writers are excluded from accessing any index defined in the collection and all other readers and writers are excluded from accessing the PDOM

step 3:

- remove the remaining phantom index entries (deleted entries left from step 3) from the indices
- *locking:* no locking necessary in step 3, since the deleted entries are already marked as phantoms and therefore are not accessible by other readers and writers

Note, that step 2 is the only *critical section* for concurrency, where all accessing processes (readers and writers) are excluded from accessing the indices and all other readers and writers are excluded from accessing the PDOM for the duration of this step.

Note also that regarding concurrency there is a violation of the ACID properties, namely the principle of isolation is not fully adhered to. As mentioned before, the commit or rollback of an update is always done in the top layer methods. Nevertheless, as soon as the locks on the indices are released after the completion of step 2, other readers and writers see not only the updated PDOM if they access it directly, but they also see the already updated indices without a commit having been issued. This is in stark contrast to what one expects, namely, that changes are only visible to other accessing processes after an explicit commit. The explanation for this behaviour is that in the Infonyte database system a commit effectuates only, that the updated state of the PDOM and affected indices is written back to secondary storage and thereby made permanent − the modified state is already visible to other readers and writers *before* the commit. A rollback on the other hand behaves in the conventional way: a rollback sets the database back to the state after the last commit, which means that all changes since then are undone. Recovery control is also done as usual in database systems: if there is a crash, the database is set back to the last committed state after a restart.

This low level of isolation is the reason why it must be emphasised, that bulk updates are very similar to transactions, but yet somewhat different, falling short of a complete implementation of the isolation principle. As we have seen, even a single update operation does not follow fully the transactional principle of isolation.

To apply the principle of isolation to its full extent would necessitate a fundamental change in the architecture of Infonyte DB. The main challenge in this task would be to overcome the contradiction of isolation and atomicity on the one hand to the live behaviour of DOM operations on the other hand, which is explicitly demanded in the DOM specification [HHW+00, HHW+03]. Live behaviour of DOM means that changes to a node in the DOM tree are immediately reflected in all references to that node.

6.4.5 Affected Node-Sets and Resulting Sets of Index Entries

In order to clarify, which node-sets are affected by the individual update operations and which sets of relevant index entries result from them, in this subchapter these node-sets and sets of index entries are identified – always assuming that the key-expressions of indices only range over the descendants of indexed nodes (refer to Subchapter 6.4.1 for the definition of *context nodes* and a description of the variables *contextEntriesBeforeUpdate[i]*, *contextEntriesAfterUpdate[i]*, *oldSubtreeEntries[i]*, and *newSubtreeEntries[i]*):

delete

context nodes	= the target node and all its ancestors
deleted nodes	= the target node and all its descendants
inserted nodes	= { }
index entries to delete (for index i)	= *contextEntriesBeforeUpdate[i] – contextEntriesAfterUpdate[i] + oldSubtreeEntries[i]*
index entries to insert (for index i)	= *contextEntriesAfterUpdate[i] – contextEntriesBeforeUpdate[i]*

replace [node]

context nodes	= the target node and all its ancestors
deleted nodes	= the target node and all its descendants
inserted nodes	= the nodes used as replacement and all their descendants
index entries to delete (for index i)	= *contextEntriesBeforeUpdate[i] – contextEntriesAfterUpdate[i] + oldSubtreeEntries[i]*
index entries to insert (for index i)	= *contextEntriesAfterUpdate[i] – contextEntriesBeforeUpdate[i] + newSubtreeEntries[i]*

replace [content]

context nodes	= the target node and all its ancestors
deleted nodes	= { }
inserted nodes	= { }
index entries to delete (for index i)	= *contextEntriesBeforeUpdate[i] – contextEntriesAfterUpdate[i]*
index entries to insert (for index i)	= *contextEntriesAfterUpdate[i] – contextEntriesBeforeUpdate[i]*

insert ['as-first' | 'as-last']

context nodes	= the target node and all its ancestors
deleted nodes	= { }
inserted nodes	= the nodes inserted including all their descendants
index entries to delete (for index i)	= $contextEntriesBeforeUpdate[i] - contextEntriesAfterUpdate[i]$
index entries to insert (for index i)	= $contextEntriesAfterUpdate[i] - contextEntriesBeforeUpdate[i]$ $+ newSubtreeEntries[i]$

insert ['before' | 'after']

context nodes	= all ancestors of the target node
deleted nodes	= { }
inserted nodes	= the nodes inserted including all their descendants
index entries to delete (for index i)	= $contextEntriesBeforeUpdate[i] - contextEntriesAfterUpdate[i]$
index entries to insert (for index i)	= $contextEntriesAfterUpdate[i] - contextEntriesBeforeUpdate[i]$ $+ newSubtreeEntries[i]$

setAttribute

context nodes	= the target node and all its ancestors
deleted nodes	= { }
inserted nodes	= { }
index entries to delete (for index i)	= $contextEntriesBeforeUpdate[i] - contextEntriesAfterUpdate[i]$
index entries to insert (for index i)	= $contextEntriesAfterUpdate[i] - contextEntriesBeforeUpdate[i]$

At first glance, it seems that for the *delete* operation the set of *index entries to insert* is always empty. But due to the flexibility of index definitions this might not be the case. In order to clarify this fact, an example of such a scenario is given:

Example 6.1: Sample XML document (with nodeID attributes for concise referencing).

```
<?xml version="1.0" encoding="UTF-8"?>
<countries nodeID="1">
         <country nodeID="2">
                  <name nodeID="3">Jamaica</name>
                  <capital nodeID="4">Kingston</capital>
         </country>
         <country nodeID="5">
                  <name nodeID="6">Japan</name>
                  <capital nodeID="7">Tokyo</capital>
         </country>
</countries>
```

Let's assume that the following index is defined on the XML document of Example 6.1:

```
<pc:index
  name="countries-by-first-country"
  match="countries"
  use="country[1]"
/>
```

So this index indexes all *countries* elements by their first *country* child element. If we create this index for the XML document in Example 6.1, there is only one *countries* element, which is indexed by its *country* child element 'Jamaica' with nodeID 2. If we now delete this *country* child element 'Jamaica', this delete operation results in the following sets of nodes and index entries (for the sake of brevity element nodes are notated with their node ID attribute as [nodeID x]):

context nodes	= { [nodeID 2], [nodeID 1] }
deleted nodes	= { [nodeID 2], [nodeID 3], [nodeID 4],
	text node 'Jamaica', text node 'Kingston' }
inserted nodes	= { }
contextEntriesBeforeUpdate[i]	= { ([nodeID 2], <[nodeID 1]>) }
contextEntriesAfterUpdate[i]	= { ([nodeID 5], <[nodeID 1]>) }
oldSubtreeEntries[i]	= { }
index entries to delete	= { ([nodeID 2], <[nodeID 1]>) }
index entries to insert	= { ([nodeID 5], <[nodeID 1]>) }

Figure 6.2 gives a graphical representation of Example 6.1 and points out the node-sets. So in this case the set of *index entries to insert* consists of the tuple ([nodeID 5], [nodeID 1]), since after the deletion the *countries* element with nodeID 1 is going to be indexed with its new first child, the *country* element 'Japan' with nodeID 5. (Remember, that index entries are tuples with this structure: (key, <list of matching nodes>)).

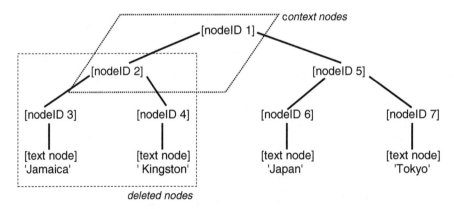

Figure 6.2: Tree relating to the sample XML document in Example 6.1 with the context nodes and deleted nodes graphically indicated.

The same argument holds in an analogous way for the *insert* operation: there the set of *index entries to delete* might not be empty.

6.5 Implementation

The Simple Update API has been developed and tested with the SUN™ Java™ JDK version 1.4.2_05. It requires the document, on which it operates, to be DOM Level 2 compliant.

All simple update operations modify only one node (called the *target node*), which helps to avoid certain update anomalies, such as, for instance, the recursive deletion of nodes, which have been deleted already (because they were a descendant of a node, on which a deep delete has been performed).

The update operations on the PDOM document are implemented by calling the respective DOM primitives as Table 6.1 illustrates:

simple update operation	DOM primitive called
insert	insertBefore( )
delete [non-attribute nodes]	removeChild( )
delete [attribute nodes]	removeAttributeNode( )
replace [node]	replaceChild( )
replace [content]	setNodeValue( )
setAttribute	setAttributeNS( )

Table 6.1: Mapping of simple updates operations to DOM primitives.

For all nodes being inserted or being used as a replacement (which again implies that they are inserted, after all, since a *replace* is identical to an *insert* followed by a *delete*), first a *deep* import of the node to insert is done (deep meaning the node and *all its descendants* are imported into the current document) before the actual update operation is performed. This import is always done, no matter if the nodes being inserted already belong to the document or not. That way all insertions and replacements are performed with copies of the nodes given as parameters in order to be consistent with the proposed XQuery updates (see Sub-chapters 3.1.1 and 3.1.3).

Note, that all *insert* operations, no matter what the *location* is, are carried out with the DOM primitive *insertBefore( )* – there is no need to use the DOM primitive *appendChild( )*.

During implementation it turned out, that it is vital to determine exactly(!) the old *context entries* and *sub-tree entries* (see Subchapter 6.4.5), otherwise some index entries might get unintentionally deleted. One mistake in the course of development was that in early versions of the API, this was handled rather generously, like, for instance, the computing of the context entries started *always* at the child of the target node, which led to the aforementioned misbehaviour.

6.5.1 Parameter Check

In order to minimise the occurrences of rollbacks, which cause a lot of expensive I/O, *all* the given parameters are always checked for validity *before* actually performing *any* update operation. For instance, if an insert is requested with a node-set as update content, every single node in the update content is checked, whether it is null or not allowed for any other reason; only if *all* parameters are ok, the update operation is carried out, otherwise an exception is raised.

The parameter checks are done by calling these *private* methods at the beginning of the respective update operation:

checkParameterDeleteLowLevel	checks if the given constellation of parameters for the subsequent call of the method *deleteLowLevel* is legal
checkParameterInsertMediumLevel	checks if the given constellation of parameters for the subsequent call of the method *insertMediumLevel* is legal
checkParameterInsertLowLevel	checks if the given constellation of parameters for the subsequent call of the method *insertLowLevel* is legal
checkParameterReplaceMediumLevel	checks if the given constellation of parameters for the subsequent call of the method *replaceMediumLevel* is legal
checkParameterReplaceLowLevel	checks if the given constellation of parameters for the subsequent call of the method *replaceLowLevel* is legal
checkParameterSetAttributeLowLevel	checks if the given constellation of parameters for the subsequent call of the method *setAttributeLowLevel* is legal

With bulk updates, the parameters for the whole sequence of update operations are checked *before any* data manipulation takes place by calling a corresponding sequence of these parameter check methods.

Beside this *static* parameter check-up, in order to support bulk updates adequately, an additional dynamic test on the parameters is carried out during the actual update operation: it is examined if the affected target is still in the document and none of its ancestors has already been removed. Otherwise the update operation on the PDOM is performed nevertheless, since this might be intended so by the user, but no update on the indices is done, because the necessary index maintenance has been carried out already when the node was removed. For this purpose the corresponding Boolean flag (which by default is set to true) will be set to false, if an ancestor of the target node has been removed from the document. Only if this Boolean flag is set to true the index updates are carried out.

6.5.2 Error Handling

If a serious error is found like, for instance, a parameter with the wrong type, an appropriate exception is thrown. Minor flaws, which have no severe impact are handled by no-operations. An example for such a minor flaw is, if during a bulk update, it is tried to delete a node, which has already been deleted or replaced by a previous update operation during the very same bulk update (such cases are not detected by the *static* parameter check). The guiding principle for the reaction of the Simple Update API to illegal or 'senseless' update requests was to correspond as much as possible to the tolerant behaviour of SQL updates in relational databases, where, for instance, also just a no-operation is performed if the attempt is made to delete a non-existing record.

6.5.3 Return Values

The methods implemented for the API usually have *Boolean* return values:
true if the method was executed successful, *false* otherwise.

The two exceptions to the rule are:

insertLowLevel this method returns the newly inserted node, because if a node-set is inserted, subsequent nodes might have to be inserted after the newly inserted node – so a way is needed to identify this newly inserted node in the calling method.

replaceLowLevel this method returns the node, which has replaced the old node, because if a node-set is used as replacement the second node in the node-set is inserted after the first node in the node-set, which has replaced the target node – so again a way is needed to identify this first node in the calling method (see also the detailed algorithm in Subchapter 6.5.6).

6.5.4 Bulk Updates

As already explained in Chapter 2 on the requirements, a *bulk update* is basically a sequence of primitive update operations, which are to be executed logically in the given order (see Subchapter 2.8). Bulk updates are implemented by the wrapper method *doBulkUpdate*, which after the aforementioned parameter check basically just goes through the list of update operations and calls the respective middle layer and bottom layer methods. After the successful processing of the whole list it issues a commit – in case an error was encountered during the processing of the list it performs a rollback.

6.5.5 Identifying the Matching Index Entries

The matching index entries for an update are found as described in the pseudo-code fragments in Listing 6.2 and 6.3. Basically it is checked for each index if the node concerned matches its domain. If yes, the respective entry is added to the set of context entries or subtree entries.

```
for each inserted node
        for each existing index i
                if the inserted node matches the domain of the index
                        add an entry to the respective set of index entries
                end if
        end for
end for
```

Listing 6.2: Algorithm for identifying the index entries for inserted nodes.

```
for each deleted node
        for each existing index i
                if the deleted node matches the domain of the index
                        add an entry to the respective set of index entries
                end if
        end for
end for
```

Listing 6.3: Algorithm for identifying the index entries for deleted nodes.

6.5.6 Detailed Algorithm

In order to describe the details of the algorithm, in the following pseudo-code listing the exact proceedings of replacing a node are thoroughly elaborated as an example. The other update operations follow the same basic approach with some minor deviations:

```
// do a deep import, because always a copy of the replacement node is used
// (even if the replacement node already belongs to the document):
importNode(replacementNode, true);

// step 1 – no locking necessary for this step:
for each index i defined in the collection
        // compute the context entries for index i before the update:
        contextEntriesBeforeUpdate[i] = indices[i].getContextEntries(targetNode, targetNodeId);
        // compute the old sub-tree entries for index i, which are to be deleted:
        oldSubtreeEntries[i] = indices[i].getSubtreeEntries(targetNode, targetNodeId);
end for

// step 2 – exclude all readers and writers from accessing any index defined in the collection:
acquireExclusiveIndicesLock( );
// exlude other readers/writers from accessing the PDOM (with standard Java synchronisation):
synchronized(doc)
        // perform the replacement:
        targetParent.replaceChild(newNode, targetNode);
        for each index i defined in the collection
        // compute the context entries for index i after the update:
        contextEntriesAfterUpdate[i] = indices[i].getContextEntries(newNode, newNodeId);
        // compute the new sub-tree entries for index i, which are to be inserted:
        newSubtreeEntries[i] = indices[i].getSubtreeEntries(newNode, newNodeId);
        // insert all the new entries (context and sub-tree) into the indices:
        contextEntriesToDelete = indices[i].insert(contextEntriesBeforeUpdate[i],
                                        contextEntriesAfterUpdate[i], newSubtreeEntries[i]);
        // mark the entries (context and sub-tree), which are to be deleted, as phantoms:
        indices[i].prepareRemove(contextEntriesToDelete, oldSubtreeEntries[i]);
        end for
        // mark the PDOM as dirty:
        markDirty(docId, getPDOM(docId));
// release lock on PDOM:
end synchronized(doc)
// release locks on indices:
releaseExclusiveIndicesLock( );

// step 3 – remove the phantom index entries (left from step 2) from the indices
// no locking necessary here, since the deleted entries are already marked as phantoms:
for each index i defined in the collection
        indices[i].doRemove( );
end for

// return the newly inserted node:
return newNode;
```

Listing 6.3: Detailed low-level algorithm for replacing a node.

Subsequently a description of the methods, which are called in the course of the algorithm, is given in a nutshell (refer to Subchapter 6.4.1 for the definitions of the *context entries* and the *sub-tree entries* of an index):

index.getContextEntries(targetNode, targetNodeId):
calculates the current context entries for *targetNode* correlating to the index, on which the method is called.

index.getSubtreeEntries(targetNode, targetNodeId):
calculates the current sub-tree entries for *targetNode* correlating to the index, on which the method is called.

index.insert(contextEntriesBeforeUpdate, contextEntriesAfterUpdate, newSubtreeEntries):
performs the following operations

1. inserts all index entries in *contextEntriesAfterUpdate*, which are not contained in *contextEntriesBeforeUpdate*, into the index, on which the method is called.

2. inserts all index entries in *newSubtreeEntries* into the index, on which the method is called.

3. calculates the set difference *contextEntriesBeforeUpdate – contextEntriesAfterUpdate* as the return value (stored subsequently in *contextEntriesToDelete*).

index.prepareRemove(contextEntriesToDelete, oldSubtreeEntries):
marks the index entries contained in *contextEntriesToDelete* and *oldSubtreeEntries* as phantom entries.

index.doRemove( ):
deletes all phantom entries from the index.

getPDOM(docId):
gets the PDOM with the given document ID *docId*.

markDirty(docId, getPDOM(docId)):
marks the PDOM with document ID *docId* as dirty.

acquireExclusiveIndicesLock( ):
requests an exclusive lock on *all* indices. As soon as this lock is granted by the database system, neither writers nor readers can access *any* index anymore. This lock prevents other accessing processes (via index) from seeing an intermediate state during the update. As long as writers or readers, which have been accessing the index before the lock has been requested, are still working on any index, this method blocks.

releaseExclusiveIndicesLock( ):
releases the locks on all indices so that other writers or readers can access the indices again.

importNode(replacementNode, true):
standard DOM primitive, which imports *replacementNode* with its attribute and the whole sub-tree beneath it.

targetParent.replaceChild(newNode, targetNode):
standard DOM primitive, which replaces the child *targetNode* of the node *targetParent* with *newNode*.

Note, that if index entries are added or removed, the affected index is marked as dirty – which is crucial for the subsequent commit, since only dirty PDOM documents and dirty indices are written back to secondary storage, if a commit is issued.

Another method worth mentioning, which has to be called by the *insertMediumLevel*, *replaceMediumLevel*, and *deleteLowLevel* methods if the respectively called DOM operation results in at least two adjacent text nodes, is the following method, which takes care of normalisation with inherent index maintenance (see also Subchapter 6.4).

mergeAdjacentTextNodes(nodeToNormalise):
merges any adjacent text nodes, which are children of the nodeToNormalise. It basically has the same effect as the DOM primitive *normalize( )*, but in contrast to this method keeps the indices consistent whilst doing so.

6.6 Alternative Solutions

This subchapter presents two alternative solutions, which might be worth reconsidering for future extensions and modifications of the Simple Update API. The title of the subchapter summarises, what kind of improvement the respective option would generate.

6.6.1 Higher Degree of Write Concurrency

During the actual implementation of the API a number of dead ends were encountered from which it was necessary to backtrack and find an alternative solution. Out of these impasses there is a particular one worth mentioning and describing (refer to Subchapter 6.4.1 for the definitions of the *context entries* and the *sub-tree entries* of an index):

The first attempt to tackle the problem of maximising the degree of concurrency was to temporarily carry out the update on the PDOM (whilst excluding other readers from accessing the indices), then calculate the new context entries and sub-tree entries *and then undo the update*. After these steps the difference of sets

$$ADD_i = contextEntriesAfterUpdate[i] - contextEntriesBeforeUpdate[i]$$

can be computed and inserted into the index i as *phantom entries* in a *non-critical section*, which means that during this phase no other accessing processes have to be blocked. Then in the following section of the algorithm the DOM update is *redone* and these phantom entries are demarcated, thereby becoming regular index entries visible to readers as soon as the lock on the indices will be released. The rest of the algorithm is identical to the presented solution. Although the degree of concurrency of this strategy is higher than in the actually implemented algorithm, this approach was dismissed because on the one hand it introduces another violation of the principle of isolation in the phase when the temporary update on the PDOM is done and undone, since in between readers who access the PDOM directly (i.e. not via index lookups but by DOM traversal) see this intermediate state and on the other hand the overhead on index maintenance turned out to be too high for these two reasons:

1. managing phantom entries during index lookups is quite expensive, so the use of phantom entries should be restricted to the bare minimum.

2. the structure index, if it was enabled at creation time of the PDOM, is updated automatically by the system on each PDOM update. So compared to the implemented algorithm there are two additional updates of the structure index – one for the undo and one the redo.

So with the actual implementation, the system is optimised for read accesses, whilst lock contentions during update operations can be higher than it would be with this alternative – if there are a lot of update operations carried out by calling the Simple Update API and few read accesses by comparison, this alternative solution might have been the better option.

In the long run a reasonable trade-off has to be found between optimising the database system for read accesses on the one hand and update operations on the other hand – the best solution might be to equip the database with the capability to configure its behaviour according to the ratio of read operations to write operations, since optimising it simultaneously for both kinds of accesses may be impracticable.

In general it has to be said that manipulations at the DOM level are always problematic, because in some application scenarios a node-set might be computed via index lookups and only some time later this node-set is actually accessed – a complex problem with a hard to find solution since it would necessitate knowing at the time of the update, which nodes are still memorised by external applications with the intention of accessing them later via that reference (see also the statement of Kha et al. in Chapter 8 'Related Work').

6.6.2 Reduced Complexity of the Algorithm

In the presented algorithm the *context entries* and *sub-tree entries* (refer to Subchapter 6.4.1 for the definitions) are treated differently: whereas the old sub-tree entries are always deleted and the new sub-tree entries are always inserted, for the context entries the differences of the set of old context entries versus the set of new context entries (and the other way round) is calculated and these difference sets are deleted and inserted appropriately. An alternative would be to first join the context entries and sub-tree entries (both old and new), then calculate the differences of the combined sets and eventually process the resulting delta in index entries accordingly. This can be expressed more formally in this way (see Subchapter 6.4.3 for a comparison):

First calculate these two unions of sets for each index i:

$$BEFORE_i = contextEntriesBeforeUpdate[i] \cup oldSubtreeEntries[i]$$

$$AFTER_i = contextEntriesAfterUpdate[i] \cup newSubtreeEntries[i]$$

Then the differences and intersection of sets would be calculated in this way:

$$REMOVE_i = BEFORE_i - AFTER_i$$

$$ADD_i = AFTER_i - BEFORE_i$$

$$KEEP_i = BEFORE_i \cap AFTER_i$$

Even if this approach would simplify the algorithm, it has been dismissed because it would induce a negative impact on the performance in the calculations of the differences and intersection of sets, since the sets, on which these calculations are carried out, are then larger compared to the actually realised solution. This negative impact is particular big if there are more sub-tree entries than context entries – which is normally the case, since the number of context nodes is *logarithmic* in the total number of nodes, whereas the number of sub-tree nodes is *linear* in the total number of nodes. So it makes sense to put up with some more complexity because of the improvement in performance – especially if one considers that the intersection of oldSubtreeEntries[i] and newSubtreeEntries[i] is always empty.

7 Correctness and Performance Evaluation

Testing and evaluating the performance of the Simple Update API are essential steps in the process of making the Simple Update API usable under real-life conditions. As it turned out, these quality assurance measures are much less trivial tasks than one is tempted to assume at first glance, even if the API consists of only two public classes and five public methods.

7.1 Analysis of the Problem of Testing and Evaluating

In order to clarify the complexity, here a concise What-Why-How-Analysis of the problem of testing and evaluating the Simple Update API is given:

What is the problem?

We want to make sure, that the Simple Update API is as *robust* as possible, which means, it shouldn't crash no matter what kind of input it is called with. Then, of course, the produced results should meet the expectations and it is mandatory to verify that they actually do. And last but not least, there should be as few *performance bottlenecks* as possible. If there are any, they should be identified and investigated, in order to work out a performance profile as a basis for a decision whether they can be tolerated or if any workarounds should and can be found for them.

Why is it a problem?

Essentially, because the number of possible database constellations and inputs is indefinite – consequently it is impossible to test and evaluate all conceivable future scenarios. The three most relevant dimensions, which will be covered and investigated up to a certain degree by testing and evaluation, are:

1. the Simple Update API should be able to update XML documents with an *arbitrary structure*, no matter whether it conforms to a DTD or schema or not.

2. the number of possible index definitions on *any* XML document or collection of XML documents is unlimited (even if the XML document consists just of the root element and accommodates no other content).

3. the number of possible sequences of update operations on *any* XML document or *any* collection of XML documents is without boundary.

Then there are other factors adding further dimensions and complexity, which will not at all or only marginally be considered in this thesis, like, for instance:

- concurrency: the Simple Update API is supposed to work correctly with several users accessing the document or collection at the same time.

- hardware: the behaviour and the outcome of calls to the Simple Update API should not depend on the underlying hardware.

- environment: the API should also be tested with other applications running, which might influence its behaviour negatively. Other circumstances on the host system should be considered as well, like, for instance, it should be able to handle situations like disk space, which runs out (an issue, which of course the database management system should take care of and react on adequately).

How do we approach the problem?

Besides static analyses of the source code, series of test cases have been constructed for *dynamic functional testing*, which can be considered as representative and typical for the future use of the Simple Update API. The run and evaluation of these test cases is highly automated, so that they can be rerun easily as *regression tests* after future modifications in order to validate, that these modifications have no negative implications or side effects and the API is still working. Additionally, more series of test cases have been constructed, which make sure that a large part of the source code has been executed and thus covered.

7.2 Static Testing

Apart from the *type checking* and *syntax checking* by the compiler and besides *walkthroughs* and other *manual static program analyses*, further static testing was greatly helped by the used programming environment (IntelliJ IDEA^{TM}). An integrated tool called 'Code Inspection' detects inconsistencies in the source code, which might point to serious errors in reasoning and should be investigated. Here is a selection of such potential weaknesses, which are reported automatically by this tool (source: online help of IntelliJ IDEA^{TM}):

unreachable code:
source code, which cannot be reached by any means.

constant conditions:
any conditions that have always only one state (for instance, only true or only false).

exceptions:
points in the source code where a RuntimeException may be thrown based on data flow analysis of the code as, for instance, method invocations that can potentially throw the null-pointer exception.

unused declarations:
classes and class members in the code that cannot be reached from any of the existing entry points.

unused method parameters:
method parameters, which are neither used in the method itself nor in any derived methods.

actual method parameter is the same constant:
methods where a value being passed to a particular parameter appears to be always the same constant.

unused method return values:
methods whose return values are never used in corresponding method calls.

method returning the same value:
methods and method hierarchies where the return value appears to be always the same constant.

empty methods:
all instances of empty methods like
- methods that are empty
- all implementations of a method are empty
- methods, which are empty themselves and are overridden only by empty methods

- methods containing only the super( ) call and passing its own parameters

redundant throws clause:
methods where an exception declared in the method signature is thrown neither by the method itself nor by its implementations or derivatives.

unused assignments:
cases where a variable value is never used after its assignment as, for instance
- the variable never gets read after assignment
- the value is always overwritten with another assignment before the next variable read
- initialisation of the variable is redundant (for one of the two reasons above)
- the variable is never used

redundant type casts:
methods having type casts, which are redundant and not necessary.

local variable or parameter can be final:
local variables or method parameters, which can be declared final.

declaration can have static modifier:
all fields, methods or classes, which may have a static modifier added to their declarations.

declaration can have final modifier:
all fields, methods or classes, that may have a final modifier added to their declarations like
- classes without subclasses
- methods that are not overridden
- fields that are initialised only once

Even if some of these flaws can be tolerated or are even intentional, it is extremely useful to have these spots automatically indicated, and then subsequently manually investigate and eliminate them or verify, that they pose no major threat of future implications. For instance, many of the methods used in the Simple Update API always return true. This can be tolerated since it makes future extensions easier, when the case might be introduced that the return value is false. On the other hand, flaws with the potential of causing major harm like, for instance, method invocations that can potentially throw the null-pointer exception should always be avoided as much as possible or at least thoroughly inspected.

The only inconsistencies reported by this tool on the *final version* of the Simple Update API are unused method return values and methods that return always the same value. All of them are intentional, because they make future extensions easier.

7.3 Dynamic Testing

On the side of dynamic testing, *functional tests* as a *black-box* testing technique and the strategy of *branch coverage* as a white-box testing method have been applied. Such a combined approach is generally considered as the economically most feasible strategy [Bal98, Lig90]. Furthermore some additional test series have been performed as *back-to-back* tests for validating the results of index maintenance.

7.3.1 Functional Testing

First each method was tested as the bottom unit, but the main focus of testing was on assessing the Simple Update API as a module – although in the course of testing some general errors in the database system were detected. Of course integration tests had to be carried out as well, like for instance, testing, if the indices are still correct after the data have been manipulated with the Simple Update API (see Subchapter 7.3.3).

A simple GUI has been programmed in order to support functional testing during development. Some constellations are very difficult (or impossible) to test with the GUI, though, so it was necessary to program a *test API* in order to support the testing of deep internals. Based on this test API, which basically provides a test driver for each public method (*delete, insert, replace, setAttribute,* and *doBulkUpdate*), a number of test cases have been invented which are dedicated to subject the Simple Update API to a black-box functionality test according to the requirements (see Chapter 2) and corresponding to the description of the public interface in this thesis (see Subchapter 6.2). All these test cases can be executed automatically. In order to facilitate the review of the results of the test runs, the outcome of each test case is written into a log file and at the end it is explicitly stated if all test cases have passed successfully or if any failures have occurred. The objective was to call the methods, which are exposed externally, within typical usage scenarios like deleting a node, replacing a node with another node or a node-set, inserting new nodes at different locations, creating new attributes and replacing the value of existing attributes, moving nodes from one position to another and so on.

The Simple Update API makes sure that after an update operation or after a sequence of update operations the document is still *well-formed*. It does not guarantee, that the document is still *valid against a schema or a DTD* (or that it was valid before the update operation, for that matter).

Since *snapshot semantics* are used, no recursions can occur. Use of snapshot semantics means, that the bindings over the input, for instance, for the target node or the update content, are made before the actual update takes place.

Some additional functional tests specialising in validating the resulting indices and PDOMs after a series of update operations by comparing the original with the modified collection are described in Subchapter 7.3.3.

7.3.2 Branch Coverage and Statement Coverage

In addition to the test cases used for functional testing described in the previous subchapter a large number of test cases have been created in order to make sure that most of the existing branches in the source code of the Simple Update API are actually covered by the testing. Reasons in favour of this particular strategy are on the one hand that *branch coverage* automatically implies *statement coverage* [Mye79] and on the other hand that branch coverage can be accomplished within a reasonable amount of time.

A method can be represented as a (directed) control flow graph, where the statements are the nodes and control flow between statements is represented by the edges [Bal98, Lig90]. Branch coverage aims at covering all the edges in this graph, whereas statement coverage tries to cover all the nodes. So, it is easy to ascertain that full branch coverage implies full statement coverage and that it also means full coverage of the source code.

All the test cases created for the purpose of branch coverage can be executed automatically as well. For constructing these test cases white-box testing was carried out, i.e. the test cases were constructed by considering the structure of the source code. Monitoring and measuring the coverage achieved by the test cases was greatly helped by the employed tool Clover [Clo04] (provided by Cenqua Pty Ltd.). After instrumenting the source code (i.e. equipping it with checkpoints and counters), it shows, which lines of the source code have been executed how many times by the test cases and also gives an overall report. Figure 6.3 (left side) shows the code coverage as it was finally achieved by running all the test cases. As it can be ascertained, on the metrics side, the Simple Update API contains 1,537 lines of code, of which are 952 non-commented lines of code. Of the 636 existing statements 575 are executed by the test cases, which amounts to a coverage of 90.4%. The percentage is worse for conditionals where only 366 out of 436 are executed, which amounts to a coverage of 83.9%. All existing 21 methods are covered by the test cases. This amounts to a total coverage of 88%.

Within practical levels of testing it would be a very difficult (if not impossible) affair to reach the remaining statements and conditionals without modifying the source code, since defensive programming principles were used as guidelines for developing, so failure conditions (e.g. nulls for parameters) are often checked at several levels in order to 'harden' the API – and the remaining uncovered statements are situated in the lower levels of the API. So most conditionals, which are left, are *if* statements, which, as an example, evaluated only to true, because the false branch is only executed in the case of error conditions which – under normal circumstances – should never occur. The statements, which are not covered by running the test cases, are mostly statements, which belong to these not executed branches of the aforementioned *if* statements. This has been easily ascertained by manual code inspection, since Clover marks every line, where not all possible states of the conditionals were covered (Clover also explicitly indicates which states are covered how many times and which states are not covered at all). Further evidence for this is the report, which Clover produces, when *if and else* statements are filtered out (see right side of Figure 6.3). In that case we have a statement coverage of 100%. The only conditional not covered is a '?' statement.

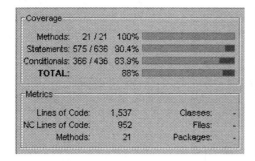 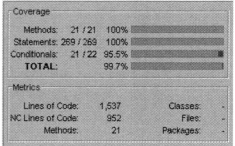

Figure 6.3: Code coverage shown by Clover with if and else statements (left) and without if and else statements (right).

It is important not to mix up *branch coverage* with the principle of *path coverage*. Whereas the applied approach of branch coverage tries to cover all branches, which exist in a program, path coverage aims for covering the logical paths in a program – however, the number of possible paths, which can be followed in the Simple Update API, is astronomical. That's already due to the fact that there are a couple of loops, for instance, when all the existing indices (which theoretically are not constrained in numbers, so there is no upper bound for the loops) are updated. So instead of trying to pursue such an unreachable objective, the described strategy was applied, which is a sensible combination of elements of black-box testing (functional tests) and white-box testing (branch coverage).

7.3.3 Verification of Index Maintenance

In addition to the preliminary and superficial testing during the development phase (like for instance, smoke tests have been performed after each modification), a test framework has been written, which makes it possible to perform varied operations on PDOMs and to efficiently achieve the test objective of validating that the indices have been maintained correctly and that the resulting PDOMs have the expected content. This test framework comprises among others the following utilities:

- Several methods have been programmed, which provide the functionality to export the contents of one or of several indices contained in a collection into a flat text file. Additionally, there exists the possibility to export the contents of PDOMs into flat text files.

- The functionality has been implemented which allows to create an identical copy of a PDOM in another collection by traversing the source PDOM in pre-order and inserting the nodes encountered on this traversal into the initially empty target PDOM by using the *insert* operation in such a way that the order and structure of the source PDOM and the target PDOM is identical in the end. One way to use this utility for testing and validating the results is as follows: first identical indices are created in both collections – the indices in the target collections being empty at first and the indices in the source collection containing the entries corresponding to the source PDOM. After performing the described copy operation and exporting the contents of the indices and PDOMs of both the source collection and the target collection, the resulting text files can be compared for equality with an appropriate tool.

- The functionality has been implemented which allows to traverse a PDOM and delete all or a randomly chosen percentage of the nodes in the target collection starting at the leaves (except the document node, of course). If this random percentage is specified as 100%, and this PDOM is the only one in a collection or if this utility is used on all the PDOMs in a collection, consequently all the indices in this collection must be empty at the end.

- The functionality has been implemented which allows to traverse two identical PDOMs in different collections simultaneously and to replace all or a randomly chosen percentage of the nodes in the target PDOM by the corresponding node in the source PDOM. If this operation is performed on two initially identical collections, after these replacement operations the defined indices *must and may only* differ in the node IDs their entries are referring to.

- The functionality has been implemented which allows to traverse two identical PDOMs in different collections simultaneously and to replace all or a randomly chosen percentage of the contents of *comments*, *text nodes*, and *processing instructions* in the target PDOM by the corresponding contents in the source PDOM. If this operation is performed on two initially identical collections, after these replacement operations the defined indices must still be identical (since the PDOMs must be identical as well).

- The functionality has been implemented which allows to traverse two identical PDOMs in different collections simultaneously and to replace all or a randomly chosen percentage of the *attribute values* in the target PDOM by the corresponding attribute values of the source PDOM. If this operation is performed on two initially identical collections, after these replacement operations the defined indices must still be identical (since the PDOMs must be identical as well).

After providing these utilities, it has been mainly a matter of choosing appropriate and representative XML documents with a good choice of content, structure, and node types as test data and creating expressive indices in order to make sure that a proper assortment of update operations are performed on a variety of PDOMs and indices defined on them.

The aforementioned utilities for exporting indices and PDOMs allow the convenient tracking and evaluation of the effects on indices and PDOMs induced by the update operations.

For all the PDOM manipulation utilities except the copy utility, it can be chosen whether they are performed as stand-alone operations by calling the *delete*, *insert*, *replace*, or *setAttribute* methods correspondingly, or whether first all operations are collected in a list and then this whole list is executed in one go as a bulk update.

Another strategy for the verification of the correct maintenance of indices by the update operations is as follows:

1. first create a collection with some suitable PDOMs and expressive indices
2. then perform a couple of update operations on these PDOMs
3. serialise the resulting PDOMs into a textual XML document
4. create PDOMs in a new collection out of the textual XML documents from step 3
5. create in this new collection the same indices as in step 1
6. then export the index contents of both collections into text files and compare these resulting text files for equality with an appropriate tool

A simplified variation of this approach is to just duplicate the collection after the update operations (instead of step 3 and 4) and then to rebuild the indices by deleting and recreating them (appropriate functionality has been programmed for automating these activities). After that step 6 can be performed analogously.

The described techniques have been carried out as data-driven tests with several XML documents which contained a variety of content, structure, and node types and consequently a variety of simple update operations and bulk updates have been performed on a series of PDOMs with a selection of indices defined on them.

All irregularities concerning the indices or the resulting PDOMs, which occurred during the test runs, were investigated and fixed, if necessary. Since the final runs showed no deviations from the specified and expected behaviour of the update operations, there is a reasonable and justifiable basis for the hypothesis, that the Simple Update API correctly keeps the indices consistent – naturally only under the restrictive assumption that the built-in functionality of Infonyte DB for the *creation* of indices works correctly as well, since rebuilding indices in duplicated collections with this built-in functionality has been done for the purpose of index maintenance verification.

7.4 Performance Evaluation

The objective of this subchapter is to evaluate the performance profile of the Simple Update API in order to identify and investigate any performance bottlenecks. The matter of analysing the overhead for index maintenance is another major concern.

The most interesting and expressive dimensions concerning update operations, XML documents, and indices are the following:

- **kind of update operation**: replace, insert, delete, etc.

- **size of an update operation**: how many nodes are inserted, how many nodes are deleted, etc.

- **structure of the document**: tabular or deeply nested

- **location of an update operation**: beginning, middle, end of the document, near the root, near the leaves

- **size of the document**

- **number and kinds of the indices defined on the collection**
- **growth of the indices induced by an update operation**

The test series developed for experimental evaluation cover these dimensions and it has been investigated, what impact a variation of some of the dimensions has on the running time. Additionally, the performance of the Simple Update API as compared to the currently used DIDO approach has been examined, and a comparison between a *replace* operation and an equivalent combination of an *insert* and *delete* operation has been performed.

Technically, performance evaluation has been carried out by instrumenting the source code with time checkpoints at all significant places. These time checkpoints are equipped with an output level, so that they can be displayed with various granularities for the test runs. For instance, if output level 1 is specified, only the overall time per individual update operation is displayed, whereas, if output level 3 is specified, even the running time at the checkpoints in the loops over the array of indices defined for the collection is displayed. Several series of performance test cases have been carried out and the generated output has been analysed. All the tests have been automated as much as possible and the test data have been pre-served for future regression tests. The findings have been supported and enhanced by using JProbe Profiler, a performance investigation tool for Java applications by Quest Software Inc., which records among others the cumulative and average time for each individual method during a test run.

7.4.1 Settings

An off-the-shelf personal computer with the following characteristics and set-up has been used for performance evaluation:

Hardware and OS

processor:	AMD Athlon XP 2000+ (1.69 GHz)
memory size:	512 Megabyte RAM
operating system:	Windows™ XP Home Edition Service Pack 1

Java set-up

JDK:	SUN™ JDK Version 1.4.2_05
initial memory heap size:	64 Megabyte
maximum memory heap size:	128 Megabyte

System settings

size of the node page cache:	3,072 nodes
size of the B*-tree cache:	2,048 pages
structure index update:	deferred
auto defragmentation threshold:	1 (auto defragmentation disabled)

As a rule, the experiments have been performed twice in a row and only the second run has been measured in order to blind out warm-up effects. The update of the structure index is deferred until the commit for all update operations of the Simple Update API, which means that the maintenance of the *signature trees* and the *document order index* (cf. Subchapter 5.5.2) poses no additional overhead on performance during the update itself. Automatic file defragmentation (cf. Subchapter 5.3) has been disabled as well in order not to let it contort the performance evaluation. Note, though, that the Java Garbage Collection is another factor left, which might potentially falsify the results.

7.4.2 Example Collections

This subchapter describes the collections used as data basis for the performance evaluation.

A significant factor concerning the overhead for index maintenance is the density of an index, which states, what proportion of nodes are indexed by a particular index in relation to the total number of nodes. For the example collections the total number of nodes and the number of nodes indexed by the individual indices are given (if relevant) so that the 'index density' can be ascertained. Full-text indices are almost always relatively dense indices.

Example I: Shakespeare's plays

As an example for a small XML document a subset of Jon Bosak's XML version of the plays of William Shakespeare (3 plays out of the original 37) has been used. Listing 7.1 shows a typical fragment of this document.

```
<?xml version="1.0"?>
<WILLIAM>
   ...
    <SCENE>
              <TITLE>SCENE VI.  Camp before Florence.</TITLE>
              <STAGEDIR>Enter BERTRAM and the two French Lords</STAGEDIR>
              <SPEECH>
                    <SPEAKER>Second Lord</SPEAKER>
                    <LINE>Nay, good my lord, put him to't; let him have his</LINE>
                    <LINE>way.</LINE>
              </SPEECH>
              <SPEECH>
                    <SPEAKER>First Lord</SPEAKER>
                    <LINE>If your lordship find him not a hilding, hold me no</LINE>
                    <LINE>more in your respect.</LINE>
              </SPEECH>
        ...
    </SCENE>
   ...
</WILLIAM>
```

Listing 7.1: Typical fragment of the XML document with the plays of Shakespeare.

The PDOM created from this data basis has the following characteristics:

total number of nodes: 26,241
used memory: 476,488 Byte

On the collection, which contains this PDOM, a full-text index and two matching multi-valued data indices have been created. Table 7.1 describes their characteristics.

domain	key	number of keys	number of nodes indexed
text# (full-text index)	(full-text index)	6,883	65,662
SPEECH	LINE	2,679	2,715
SPEECH	SPEAKER	93	2,715

Table 7.1: Indices defined on the collection containing the plays of Shakespeare.

Additionally, there exist another three multi-valued data indices, which don't match the PDOM with the plays of Shakespeare at all. Besides, the collection contains four other very small PDOMs.

Example II: DBLP

In order to measure performance under real-life conditions with a realistic database size a PDOM has been created from the *DBLP XML document of bibliographical entries*. The XML document itself has been downloaded on the 27th of July 2004 from the DBLP web site [DBLP] and the PDOM created from it has the following characteristics:

Total number of nodes: 11,597,801
Used memory: 180,994,286 Byte

The collection contains a full-text index and several multi-valued data indices, which represent a fair blend of *dense* and *sparse* indices. The details are given in Table 7.2.

domain	key	number of keys	number of nodes indexed
text# (full-text index)	(full-text index)	976,350	16,691,125
article	author	88,408	196,136
book	editor	85	98
book	author	854	1,064
author	.	347,808	1,218,416
article	@mdate	509	198,198
article	@key	198,198	198,198

Table 7.2: Indices defined on the collection containing the DBLP PDOM.

Additionally, there exist two multi-valued data indices, which don't match the DBLP PDOM at all. Besides the DBLP PDOM, the collection contains four other very small PDOMs. Listing 7.2 shows a typical fragment of the DBLP document.

```
<?xml version="1.0"?>
<dblp>
      ...
      <article mdate="2002-01-03" key="tr/gte/TR-0169-12-91-165">
            <ee>db/labs/gte/TR-0169-12-91-165.html</ee>
            <author>Frank Manola</author>
            <title>Object Data Language Facilities for Multimedia Data Types.</title>
            <journal>GTE Laboratories Incorporated</journal>
            <volume>TR-0169-12-91-165</volume>
            <month>December</month>
            <year>1991</year>
            <url>db/labs/gte/index.html#TR-0169-12-91-165</url>
            <cdrom>GTE/MANO91a.pdf</cdrom>
      </article>
      ...
</dblp>
```

Listing 7.2: Typical fragment of the DBLP XML document.

Example III: synthetic XML documents

In order to have control over the structure of an XML document, a utility has been programmed, which is able to create synthetic XML documents with configurable size, depth and fan-out. Such a synthetically generated document consists of a number of person elements (or *records*), which contain several sub-elements, among others a <father> and a <mother> element, both of which can contain a <father> and a <mother> element again and therefore can be nested at will. Listing 7.3 shows a typical fragment of such a document.

```
<?xml version="1.0"?>
<persons>
          ...
          <person ID='_100000'>
                  <login>ßBUuW</login>
                  <password>BFVCTuJm</password>
                  <lastname>wpq yrlk</lastname>
                  <firstname>tEVzqKHma</firstname>
                  ...
                  <father generation='1'> IdMFLFemTvYjExSt
                          <father generation='2'>NZVCuQihewX</father>
                  </father>
                  <mother generation='1'> DPJPfR
                          <mother generation='2'> MFqBVdDN </mother>
                  </mother>
          </person>
          ...
</persons>
```

Listing 7.3: Typical fragment of a synthetically generated XML document.

The collection contains a full-text index and several multi-valued data indices, which represent a fair blend of *dense* and *sparse* indices. Table 7.3 gives the details for a synthetically generated document with 50 records and 12 levels of nesting.

domain	key	number of keys	number of nodes indexed
text# (full-text index)	(full-text index)	76,146	110,438
person	lastname	50	50
person	@ID	50	50
father	@generation	10	51,150
mother	@generation	10	51,150

Table 7.3: Indices defined on the collection containing the synthetic documents.

Besides the synthetically generated document, the collection contains four other very small PDOMs.

7.4.3 Replace Versus DIDO

The objective of the first series of experiments is to investigate the improvement in performance achieved by using the Simple Update API as compared to the DIDO (Document In, Document Out) approach mentioned in the introduction of this thesis (which is currently used in Infonyte DB whenever an XML document is modified). As data basis for this evaluation served the XML document with the plays of Shakespeare (see Subchapter 7.4.2 – Example I).

The DIDO approach means in essence a replacement of the original document with the modified document, so this replacement of a document was mimicked by a *replace[node]* operation on the root of the document. Since it is not possible to replace a root node with the Simple Update API, the original root node has been nested into an artificial new root. The expected result of this test is that the DIDO approach should be 1 to 2 times faster than the *replace[node]* operation, since with the *replace[node]* operation the document has to be traversed between 4 to 5 times, whereas the DIDO approach needs only 3 passes. Table 7.4 reports on the results of several tests runs.

test run	replacing the document with the DIDO approach [milliseconds]	replace[node] of the original root [milliseconds]	ratio replace[node] / DIDO [percent]
1	2,969	2,844	95.79
2	2,906	2,922	100.55
3	2,890	2,891	100.03

Table 7.4: Running times *replace[node]* versus *DIDO*.

The running times are varying a bit but the tendency is obvious: the performance is nearly equal and therefore confirming the expectation.

Note that this scenario in a way represents the worst case for the Simple Update API if competing with the DIDO approach, since in most other usage scenarios only fragments of the document are modified and not the whole document is replaced. Therefore it can be concluded that – if a single update operation is performed – it is probably always advisable to do this via the Simple Update API. Matters might be different if the usage scenario consists of several successive update operations. Then, in some cases the DIDO approach might yield better performance. Suppose, for instance, that in the running example the *replace[node]* operation for some reason is performed several times. Table 7.5 shows the accumulated time needed for repeatedly executing this operation, when in comparison the (single) replacement of the document with the DIDO approach took 2,953 milliseconds.

number of replace[node] operations	accumulated time needed [milliseconds]	
	commit disabled	commit enabled
1	1,797	3,047
2	2,969	5,266
3	4,250	7,188
4	5,984	9,859

Table 7.5: Accumulated times for multiple *replace[node]* operations.

As can be deduced from Table 7.5, the DIDO approach is faster if two or more subsequent *replace[node]* operations on the root of the document are performed, no matter if a commit is issued after each operation or only at the end. However, since this is again the worst case for the Simple Update API, the number of subsequent update operations, for which the Simple Update API is faster, is usually much higher in practical average cases. For instance, it takes only 844 milliseconds to replace 100 <SPEECH> elements with the *replace[node]* operation, which is less than a third of the time needed by the DIDO approach.

In order to ascertain how the running time depends on the size of the replaced document, the test runs described in Table 7.4 (with only 3 plays of Shakespeare) have been carried out on an XML document with the complete plays of Shakespeare, placed in an otherwise identical collection.

The PDOM created from this data basis is an order of magnitude bigger and has the following characteristics:

total number of nodes: 327,009
used memory: 6,286,414 Byte

Table 7.6 gives the results of the tests runs on this PDOM.

test run	replacing the document with the DIDO approach [milliseconds]	replace[node] of the original root [milliseconds]	ratio replace[node] / DIDO [percent]
1	19,859	33,765	170.02
2	17,453	30,375	174.04
3	19,125	30,844	161.28

Table 7.6: Running times *replace[node]* versus *DIDO* for the complete plays of Shakespeare.

In this case, the *replace[node]* operation takes 61 to 74 percent longer than the DIDO approach, which is still within the expectation. It can be concluded that the larger the document is the more favourable it is to use the DIDO approach.

It has also been investigated, how the number of indices defined in a collection influences the running time of replacing a whole document. For that purpose, collections have been created with the 3 indices described in Table 7.1 duplicated 10 to 60 times and a single replacement of the document has been carried out. Figure 7.1 shows the outcome of these experiments. It can be observed that for the *replace[node]* operation after a linear increase from 3 to 30 indices the running time remains at nearly the same level, whereas with the DIDO approach there is a linear increase from 3 to 120 indices and after that performance degrades dramatically. So the conclusion can be drawn that the more indices are defined on a collection the more favourable it is to use the Simple Update API.

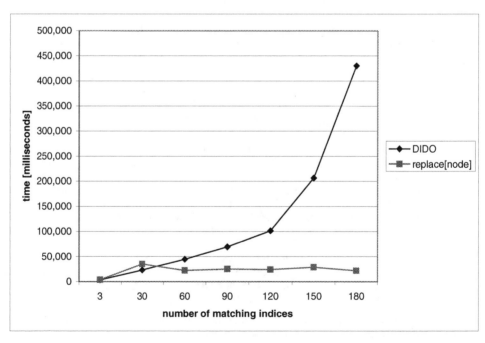

Figure 7.1: Time needed for replacing a whole document with the commit enabled and various numbers of indices defined for the collection (the diagram is very similar with the commit disabled).

7.4.4 Detailed Evaluation

For a detailed evaluation of the running time the *replace* operation was analysed, since it is equivalent to an insertion followed by a deletion and therefore the results give some clues on these operations as well. The data basis used was the DBLP PDOM (see Subchapter 7.4.2 – Example II). There an author of an article has been replaced by another author. Since the commit consumes more than 99 percent of the total time, it has been disabled in order to evaluate the time consumption of the core operations in the Simple Update API.

Without the commit the replacement operation took 360 milliseconds in total (including the parameter check). Table 7.7 gives the detailed output of the JProbe Profiler for the methods called in the bottom layer method *replaceLowLevel* (see Subchapter 6.5.6 for a description of the algorithm and the called methods) in descending order of the total time needed.

method name	calls	total method time [milliseconds]	(percent)	average method time [milliseconds]	(percent)
Index.doRemove( )	9	302	(94.0 %)	34	(10.4 %)
Index.insert(...)	9	17	(5.2 %)	2	(.6 %)
UpdateMan.replaceLowLevel(...)	1	1	(.3 %)	1	(.3 %)
Index.getContextEntries(...)	18	1	(.2 %)	0	(.0 %)
Index.getSubtreeEntries(...)	18	1	(.2 %)	0	(.0 %)
Index.prepareRemove(...)	9	0	(.1 %)	0	(.0 %)
getPDOM(...)	1	0	(.0 %)	0	(.0 %)
importNode(...)	1	0	(.0 %)	0	(.0 %)
replaceChild(...)	1	0	(.0 %)	0	(.0 %)
markDirty(...)	1	0	(.0 %)	0	(.0 %)
getDID(...)	1	0	(.0 %)	0	(.0 %)
acquireExclusiveIndicesLock( )	1	0	(.0 %)	0	(.0 %)
releaseExclusiveIndicesLock( )	1	0	(.0 %)	0	(.0 %)
Total:		**328**	**(100 %)**		

Table 7.7: Time needed by the methods called in *replaceLowLevel*.

The lion's share of the time needed for this replacement operation is due to the method *Index.doRemove( )*, which removes the phantom entries from the respective index. This method is called 9 times, once for each existing index and takes up 94.0 percent of the total time in *replaceLowLevel*. The second most expensive method, *Index.insert(...)*, inserts the new entries into the respective index, converts the context entries, which are subsequently to be deleted, into phantom entries, and consumes 5.2 percent of the total time. The time needed by the other called methods is negligible, for instance, the DOM operation *Node.replaceChild(...)* takes less than 500 microseconds, which means that the running time of *replaceLowLevel* is nearly all spent on index maintenance.

7.4.5 Varying the Number of Indices in the Collection

As another series of experiments with the objective of going deeper into the matter of overhead caused by index maintenance, several collections have been created with both the full-text index and the multi-valued data index with the domain 'article' and the key 'author' (see Table 7.2) duplicated 5 to 20 times and then the same *replace* operation as in the previous subchapter has been performed on the DBLP PDOM. Figure 7.2 shows the results for the total time needed for *replaceLowLevel* and the most time-consuming called methods and serves as further confirmation that index maintenance is the dominant factor for the running time of the replace operation, since the running time grows linearly in the number of indices with an identical update operation performed on identical base data.

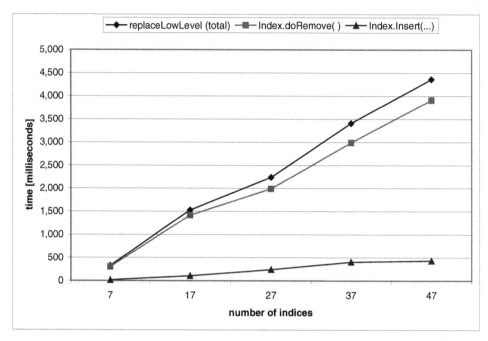

Figure 7.2: Running time of *replaceLowLevel, Index.doRemove( ),* and *Index.insert(...)* with various numbers of indices defined for the collection.

7.4.6 Varying the Growth of the Indices

In order to ascertain what impact the growth of an index induced by an update operation has on performance, a further series of experiments has been developed, which also use the collections with various numbers of indices defined on them as in the previous subchapter. On each of these collections 6 single *replace[content]* operations have replaced the value of a text node with a new text value consisting of 1 to 1,000 artificially generated words, thereby inserting equally many new keys into the full-text indices. The old text value consisted of a single word. It is expected that the running time increases *logarithmically* in the number of new keys, because the lookup for a key in an index is done via binary search, which is the most time-consuming operation when inserting a new entry into an index. Figure 7.3 shows that the result fully meets the expectations independently from the number of indices defined on the collection.

A deeper analysis of the running time yields that the largest part of the performance is spend on adding the new entries to the B*-tree indices. For instance, if 200 new keys are inserted into the collection with 17 indices, 99.3 percent of the total running time is used up by the corresponding system routine.

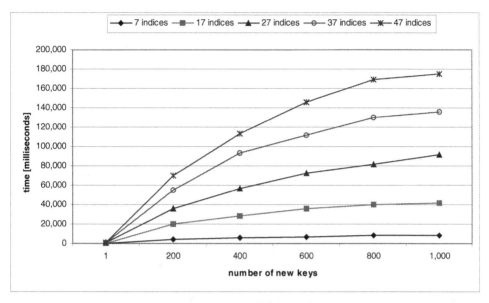

Figure 7.3: Running time of *replace[content]* operations, which insert new keys into collections with various numbers of indices defined on them.

7.4.7 Replace Versus Insert/Delete

On the aforementioned DBLP collections with various numbers of indices another series of experiments has been conducted with the objective to ascertain the difference in running time between a *replace* operation and the equivalent sequence of an *insert* operation followed by a *delete* operation. For this purpose an author of an article has been replaced by another author by both a replace operation and a combination of an insertion and a deletion. The same comparison has been performed for the replacement of the title of an article with another title. Naturally, the *replace* operation is expected to be more efficient because of compensation effects like, for instance, having to calculate the context entries (refer to Subchapter 6.4.1 for the definitions of the *context entries* of an index) only once for each index. Figure 7.4 depicts the benefit achieved by using the replace operation. For the replacement of the author the replace operation needs only between 57 and 63 percent of the time consumed by the equivalent insert/delete combination, and for the replacement of the title the percentage is between 51 and 58, thereby meeting the expectations.

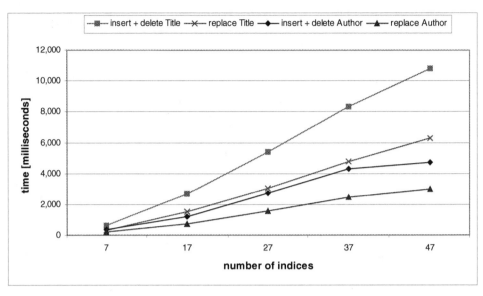

Figure 7.4: Running time of *replace* and the equivalent combination of *insert* and *delete* with various numbers of indices defined for the collection.

A deeper analysis with the JProbe Profiler yields that the advantage of the replace operation is based on the lesser time consumption for the methods *Index.insert(...)* and *Index.doRemove( )*, which use up the lion's share of the total running time. Table 7.8 gives the time needed for the collection with 17 indices.

	AUTHOR Index.insert(...) [milliseconds]	AUTHOR Index.doRemove() [milliseconds]		TITLE Index.insert(...) [milliseconds]	TITLE Index.doRemove() [milliseconds]
insert	643	0		970	0
delete	0	505		0	1693
insert + delete	643	505		970	1693
replace	633	44		2	1462

Table 7.8: Time needed by *Index.insert(...)* and *Index.doRemove( )* during replacement.

7.4.8 Varying the Depth and the Fan-Out

Since an XML document can be represented as a tree, the data size can vary in two directions: depth-wise and breadth-wise. Thus, apart from the density of the tree, *depth* and *fan-out* are two important structural parameters. In order to see what implications are caused by a change in depth or fan-out, several series of experiments have been performed on PDOMs generated from the synthetic XML documents (see Subchapter 7.4.2 – Example III) with a variety of values for these two parameters.

The first such PDOM has the following characteristics:

Number of records (equals maximal fan-out):   50
Depth: 12
Total number of nodes: 308,452
Used memory: 2,670,825 Byte

First a top-level record has been deleted, which induced the removal of 6,169 nodes in total. The overall running time of *deleteLowLevel* was 118 milliseconds, 50.1 percent of which was consumed by the *Index.getSubtreeEntries(...)* method call, 45.6 percent by the *Index.doRemove( )* method call, and 2.9 percent by the *Index.prepareRemove(...)* method call. The same experiment with depth 10 and depth 7 resulted in similar proportions, whereas with depth 14, when much more nodes are deleted, the *Index.doRemove( )* method call takes up 72.6 percent and the *Index.getSubtreeEntries(...)* method call 26.7 percent.

Then a synthetic PDOM with a depth of 77 has been created in order to measure the impact of the factor *depth* on performance. Experiments, during which nodes at various levels have been deleted, replaced and inserted, showed no significant influence of the depth of a node on the performance of the update operations. An explanation is that the deeper down the update operation takes place, the smaller is the set of sub-tree entries on the one hand, but the larger is the set of context entries on the other hand.

For a variance in *fan-out* synthetic PDOMs with 50, 500, 5,000, and 50,000 records have been created and the last record has been replaced by a single node (the last record in order to avoid the positional effects exposed in Subchapter 7.4.9). As it turned out, varying the fan-out has hardly any impact on the running time of an update operation since the total time needed for the replacement was always less than 125 milliseconds. The size of the collections, which contained these PDOMs, ranged from 18,502 to 18,499,997 nodes. Since the running time was in a similar range for all collections, it can also be concluded that the time needed by an update operation is fairly independent from the total number of nodes in a collection.

7.4.9 Updates at Various Positions in the Document

In order to investigate how the performance of an update operation depends on the position of the updated document fragment, a synthetic document (see Subchapter 7.4.2 – Example III) with the following characteristics has been created:

Number of records: 50,000
Depth: 3
Total number of nodes: 1,850,002
Used memory: 17,029,733 Byte

The collection contains a set of indices as given in Table 7.3.

Then *replace[node]*, *replace[content]*, *delete*, *insert*, and *setAttribute* operations have been performed at different locations within this document. Figure 7.5 shows the outcome.

As can be ascertained from Figure 7.5, the running time of the *replace[node]*, *delete*, and *insert* operations is the higher the closer the updated document fragment is to the beginning of the document. Further investigation shows that a predominant part of the running time is spent on executing the respective DOM primitive, unless the update is performed near the end. For instance, 98.9 percent of the total running time for a replacement at position 10,000 is spent on the *replaceChild* DOM primitive and 93.1 percent in case of a replacement at position 30,000, whereas it is only .1 percent at position 50,000. This is due to the fact that the *child order index* (cf. Subchapter 5.5.2) is *always* automatically recalculated when executing the DOM primitive and the child order index values for all siblings *after* the manipulated node have to be updated, which necessitates loading them into main memory. This also explains why the running time of the *setAttribute* and *replace[content]* operations is next to nothing, no matter at which position the update operation takes place: these update operations have no impact on the child order index, so there is no need to recalculate it.

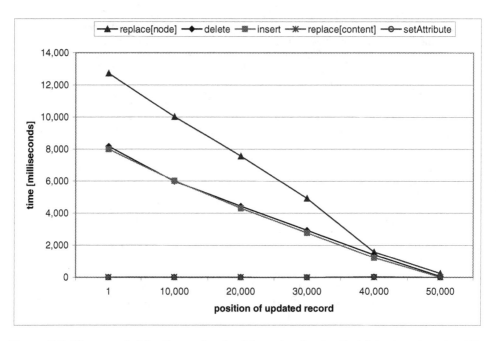

Figure 7.5: Time needed for the *replace[node], replace[content], delete, insert,* and *setAttribute* operations at different locations within the document (commit is disabled).

7.4.10 Varying the Size of an Update

In order to learn about the running time in relation to the number of nodes affected by an update operation, series of experiments have been conducted on a synthetically generated PDOM (see Subchapter 7.4.2 – Example III) with the following characteristics:

Number of records (equals maximal fan-out):	5,000
Depth:	7
Total number of nodes:	1,085,001
Used memory:	9,304,190 Byte

The collection contains a set of indices as given in Table 7.3. Each record is represented by a *person* element and consists of 217 nodes in total.

The following experiments have been conducted with x adopting each value from the set {1; 400; 800; 1,200; 1,600; 2,000}:

- Delete x records from the end of the PDOM.

- Append x new records at the end of the PDOM (by using the *insert[after]* operation).

- Replace the record at the end of the PDOM with x other records.

- Replace the value of the *ID* attribute of x records (by using the *setAttribute* operation).

- Replace the text content of the sub-element *lastname* in x records.

Except when replacing attribute values or contents of nodes, all update operations have been carried out at the end of the document in order to avoid the negative impact on performance caused by the automatic maintenance of the child order index (cf. Subchapter 7.4.9), which would contort the results otherwise. Figure 7.6 reports on the outcome of the experiments.

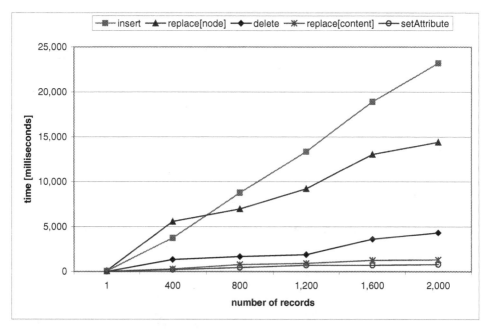

Figure 7.6: Running time of the update operations in relation to the number of affected nodes.

For all update operations the running time is linear or better in relation to the number of nodes affected. The correlation is exceedingly good in the case of the *setAttribute* and *replace[content]* operations, since they don't trigger a recomputation of the child order index.

7.4.11 Volume Tests with Bulk Updates

In order to determine the performance profile of the Simple Update API when dealing with large update volumes the utilities programmed for the verification of index maintenance (see Subchapter 7.3.3) have been re-used on the PDOM with the plays of Shakespeare (see Subchapter 7.4.2 – Example I) for a series of experiments.

One experiment was to delete in a bulk update all of the nodes of the PDOM (except the document node) starting at the leaves. It took 99 seconds to delete 26,239 nodes, which results in an average of 3.77 milliseconds per node.

Another experiment was to clone this PDOM into a different collection and then to traverse the two identical PDOMs simultaneously and to replace in a bulk update all of the nodes in the cloned PDOM by the corresponding node in the source PDOM (again starting at the leaves). Contrary to expectations, it took only 43 seconds to replace all 26,241 nodes, which is less than half of the time needed for deleting as many nodes and results in an average of 1.64 milliseconds per node. This is due to the fact that in the case of delete operations the DOM primitive performed on the PDOM (*removeChild*) takes up 79.2 percent of the total time, whereas in the case of replacement operations the DOM primitive (*replaceChild*) consumes only .6 percent of the total time.

These two experiments can serve as an average case analysis, since in both cases nodes have been manipulated at all positions in the document and at all nesting levels and thereby affecting document fragments with different granularities.

For all experiments so far, the configuration of main memory usage by PDOMs and indices has been as follows: the size of the node page cache has been set to 3,072 nodes, and the size of the B*-tree cache to 2,048 pages. This kind of setting mimics working on a database with normal size and sufficient main memory available. In order to simulate the usage scenario of a very large database in an environment with insufficient main memory available, both of these parameters have been set to 200, with the result that the aforementioned bulk updates took more than twice as long due to the additionally induced disk I/O: running time was 204 seconds for the deletion and 107 seconds for the replacement.

7.4.12 Conclusions from the Performance Evaluation

Very early in the course of the performance evaluation, it turned out that the lion's share of the time needed is spent on committing the updates on the PDOMs and the indices – at least when operating on large XML documents. For instance, in the case of replacing a node in the DBLP PDOM the running time of the commit is two orders of magnitude higher than for any of the other components of the update operation. Note that this fact constitutes a strong case to use *bulk updates* (see Subchapter 2.8 for a description) whenever a sequence of update operations is performed, since bulk updates issue just one commit at the end of the sequence of update operations in contrast to a sequence of *single* updates, which will commit for each individual update operation. The fact that the commit on large PDOMs causes a major overhead is the reason why for many experiments the commit part has been disabled by commenting it out in order to ascertain the performance of the update operations themselves (then naturally mainly performed in transient memory).

The performance evaluation showed furthermore that the update operations are scalable both in the total number of nodes in the database and in the number of nodes affected by the update operation. A negative result is that – due to the automatic maintenance of the child order index – the running time of an update operation depends very much on the location where it is performed.

Another finding is that in many cases the largest part of the running time of an update operation is used up by routines on the indices provided by the database system such as putting new entries into an B*-tree index, removing phantom entries from an index and so on. This serves as an argument that the implemented algorithm indeed optimises performance, since it minimises the use of such index routines by first calculating the delta in index entries induced by an update operation and afterwards just processing this delta.

8 Related Work

Igor Tatarinov et al. propose a set of XQuery extensions for updates in [TIHW01], which comprises the update operations *delete, insert, replace, insertBefore, insertAfter,* and – in contrast to the work presented here – also a *rename* operation. The *insert* operation is only meant for inserting *into* a target *at the end of the existing content* of this target – to insert *before* or *after* a target the *insertBefore* or *insertAfter* operations have to be used. Creation and modification of attributes is covered in this proposal by the *insert* and *replace* operations.

Patrick Lehti also proposes an extension for updates to the XQuery language in [Leh01], which consists of an *Insert*, a *Delete*, a *Replace* and a *Rename* expression. Like in [TIHW01], creation and modification of attributes is covered in his proposal by the *Insert* and *Replace* operations, too. Single updates can be grouped into a composition of several updates. He has implemented an update processor as an extension of an existing XQuery processor, which is able to execute his proposed update operations. Furthermore he has put together an extensive list of requirements on an XML update language and a list of use cases for XML updates.

Despite its obvious shortcomings, which have been pointed out in Subchapter 3.2.8, the XUpdate proposal has been implemented in a number of XML repositories like eXist [Mei02, Mei04, CRZ03], a native XML database system developed by Wolfgang Meier, and Xindice [XIND04], the XML database project of the Apache Software Foundation.

Regarding the complexity of efficiently implementing indices in XML databases the following statement of Kha et al. [KYU01] is quite interesting: „due to the complex structure of XML documents, an index that is efficient for both update and retrieval may not available. One of alternatives [sic!] is building two separate indices such that one is suitable when update is frequent; the other is better at query processing. In this case, a transformation mechanism between the indexing structures is need [sic!] to be developed."

More related work has already been discussed in Chapter 4 'Indices in XML Databases', particularly in Subchapter 4.2 'Indices on Structure'.

9 Summary and Conclusions

This thesis made the following contributions:

The Simple Update API for the native XML database management system Infonyte DB has been designed, implemented, tested, and evaluated, which provides the necessary function- ality to perform fine-grained, node-wise, and *index-aware* update operations on fragments of XML documents. Following the style of the emerging XQuery standard, these update opera- tions supply an abstract high-level interface for performing write accesses to the database. The update operations are *index-aware* in the sense that the existing user-defined indices on values are automatically maintained without any need of manual intervention. The underlying algorithm, which is basically the same for all operations, calculates the delta in index entries induced by the update operation and inserts respectively deletes entries from the indices appropriately. The applied techniques for both the update operations themselves and the index maintenance have been kept very simple and straightforward. The update operations with their inherent index maintenance are equipped with transactional capabilities, but make some compromises on the principle of isolation. The functionality and performance of the implemented API has been systematically and thoroughly tested and these tests have been automated to a high degree in order to support future regression testing. Furthermore the two most prominent existing proposals for XML updates, namely the W3C's proposed extension of XQuery with operations for data manipulation and XUpdate (a proposition by the XML:DB initiative) have been analysed and their weaknesses and shortcomings have been dis- cussed. In addition, the various ways of realising indices in XML databases have been inves- tigated.

As it turned out, updates with transparent index maintenance in XML databases present a much more complex issue than, for instance, in relational databases, because in XML data- bases it is not only required to update and insert *data*, but also to update and insert *structure (i.e. context)* which make it much more difficult to determine the indices affected by an up- date. In relational databases, with their rigid structure and strict separation between structure and data, the structure of the data is known and cannot change by an update of the data, so this task (to determine which indices are affected by the update and have to be maintained) can be relatively easy be performed by referring to the structure information in the dictionary. The occasional changes on the *structure of the data* (also often called *metadata*) are usually handled in respect to index maintenance by a recomputation of the indices.

The main challenge for the index maintenance in XML databases is the fact that the structure of the data is not known beforehand and might change at any time – there is a lack of fixed schema. The presented algorithm does not restrict the current or future structure of the in- dexed XML documents in any way, but functions efficiently and correctly, as long as the range of the indices (= *use expression* – see Subchapter 5.5.1) is limited to the indexed node and its descendants.

The performance evaluation showed on the positive side that the update operations are scalable both in the total number of nodes in the database and in the number of nodes af- fected by the update operation. As a negative result it turned out that the running time of an update operation heavily depends on the location where it is performed.

Future work:

There remains a number of unsolved issues, which might be worth investigating, like, for in- stance, referential integrity was not a concern in this thesis and responsibility for it is left to the accessing applications for the time being, which is in stark contrast to conventional data- base systems, where the DBMS takes care of this issue and makes sure that no inconsisten- cies in this regard can occur.

Staying in the same category, the validity of intra-document or inter-document references like KEY/KEYREF and ID/IDREF identity constraints are issues, which are currently ignored by the Simple Update API.

Other interesting extensions for the Simple Update API might be inherent Schema and DTD validation – both issues, which were left out in this thesis.

Furthermore the low level of isolation regarding concurrency, as it is described in Sub-chapters 6.3 and 6.4, is a weakness of the current solution, which should be addressed in future versions of Infonyte DB.

Glossary

Ancestor
An *ancestor* node of a node A is any node above A in a tree model of a document, where 'above' means 'toward the root'.

API
An *Application Programming Interface* is a set of functions, methods, variables, constants, and other objects, which can be used to access some functionality.

Atomic value
An *atomic value* is a value in the value space of an XML Schema atomic type, as defined in [Fal01] (that is, a simple type that is not a list type or a union type).

Candidate Recommendation
A *Candidate Recommendation* is a W3C document type, which follows the 'last call' Working Draft and precedes the Proposed Recommendation. It is an explicit call to those outside of the related Working Groups or the W3C itself for implementation and technical feedback.

Child
A *child* is an immediate descendant node of a node.

Context item
The *context item* is the item currently being processed in a path expression. An item is either an atomic value or a node.

Context node
When the context item is a node, it can also be referred to as the *context node*.

Context position
The *context position* is the position of the context item within the sequence of items currently being processed in a path expression.

Context size
The *context size* is the number of items in the sequence of items currently being processed in a path expression.

Descendant
A *descendant* node of any node A is any node below A in a tree model of a document, where 'above' means 'toward the root'.

Document order
The *document order* is defined on all the nodes in a document. The *document order* is a total ordering, although the relative order of some nodes is dependent on the implementation. Informally, *document order* is the order returned by a pre-order, depth-first, left-to-right traversal of the data model.

DOM
The *Document Object Model* [HHW+00, HHW+03] is a platform independent interface for accessing HTML and XML documents usable from within programming and scripting languages. The DOM presents documents in an object-oriented fashion.

DTD
Document Type Definitions are a schema specification method for SGML and XML documents. *DTDs* are either contained in the document or belong to its external subset and are then referenced from within the document's document type declaration per URI.

Element
Each document contains one or more *elements*, the boundaries of which are either delimited by start-tags and end-tags, or, for empty *elements* by an empty-element tag. Each *element* has a type, identified by name, and may have a set of attributes. Each attribute has a name and a value.

Empty sequence
A sequence containing zero items is called an *empty sequence*.

Garbage collection
A technique used in Java to eliminate objects that are no longer needed by the program. When no other objects or variables are accessing an object, it can be safely removed, freeing memory allocated to the object.

Inter-document references
Inter-document references are references that refer to nodes that do not reside in the same XML document as the reference itself.

Intra-document references
Intra-document references are references that reside in the same XML document as the nodes they reference.

Item
An *item* is either an atomic value or a node.

Java
Java is a modern object oriented programming language. *Java* classes compile into Java-bytecode. This code can be executed on any platform that implements the *Java* Virtual Machine (JVM).

Local name
A *local name* is the local part of a qualified name. This is called the local part in the W3C Recommendation on Namespaces in XML [BHL99].

Location path
In XPath, a *location path* is used for addressing one or more nodes of a given XML object tree. In XQuery a path starts from the root node and has one or more location steps.

Location step
In XPath, a *location step* selects a set of nodes of a given XML object tree. It contains an axis, a node test and optional predicates (filter expressions).

Namespace prefix
A *namespace prefix* is a string that associates an element or attribute name with a namespace URI in XML.

Namespace URI
A *namespace URI* is a URI that identifies an XML namespace. Strictly speaking, this actually is a namespace URI reference. This is called the namespace name in Namespaces in XML [BHL99].

Namespaces

Namespaces are a W3C activity concerning XML to enable documents to use names speci-fied in foreign DTDs. A namespace declaration within an XML document points to a *name-space* 'ns' via a URI. Thus the names contained in this *namespace* are available in the form 'ns:name' within a specific part of the document tree.

Native XML Database

One possible definition (developed by members of the XML:DB mailing list): *Native XML Databases* have an XML document as its fundamental unit of (logical) storage, just as a rela-tional database has a row in a table as its fundamental unit of (logical) storage. *Native XML Databases* are not required to have any particular underlying physical storage model. For example, it can be built on a relational, a hierarchical, or an object-oriented database, or use a proprietary storage format such as, for instance, indexed and compressed files.

Node

A *node* is an instance of one of the seven *node* kinds defined in the XQuery 1.0 and XPath 2.0 Data Model [FMM+01]: document, element, attribute, text, namespace, processing in-struction, and comment. In DOM this definition is somewhat different, for instance there are no namespace *nodes* in DOM.

Node-set

A node s*et* in XML can contain attributes and is ordered. In order to make this distinction more evident in this thesis the term *node-set* is used instead of node set.

Parent

A *parent* is an immediate ancestor node of a node.

Proposed Recommendation

A *Proposed Recommendation* is a W3C document type, which represents consensus within the developing group and which has been proposed by the director to be discussed in the consultative committee.

Qualified name

A *qualified name (QName)* is the name of an element or attribute defined as a local name, which is optionally preceded by a namespace prefix and colon character.

Recommendation

A *Recommendation* is a W3C document type, which represents consensus with the W3C and possesses the certification of the director. The W3C considers the ideas or technologies specified by the *recommendation* as the basis for a widespread development and support of the W3C mission.

Root node

The *root node* is the unique node that is not a child of any other node. On the other hand all other nodes are children or other descendants of the *root node*. Synonyms of *root node* are *document node* or *document element.*

Scalability

The ability to maintain high performance levels despite a significant increase in database size or workload.

Schema

A *schema* specifies rules for how XML document elements, attributes, and other data are defined and logically related in an XML-compliant document. It can contain definitions of doctypes and collections.

Semistructured data
Semistructured data are data with an irregular or changing organisation (see also Appendix A2).

Sequence
A *sequence* is an ordered collection of zero or more items. Sequences never contain other sequences – if sequences are combined, the result is always a "flattened" sequence.

Sibling
Two nodes are *siblings* if and only if they have the same parent node.

Tree
A *tree* is a data structure consisting of nodes, which may contain other nodes via its branches. Unlike a tree in nature, the root node is usually represented at the top of the structure and does not have a parent node. All other nodes have a single parent. Nodes having no child nodes are called leaf nodes. An XML document represents a tree structure.

URI
A *Universal Resource Identifier* is either a URL or a URN. A URI is a way of identifying content in the web, whether it is a page of text, a video or sound clip, an image, or a program.

URL
A *Universal Resource Locator* is a unique address of a document or a resource on the Internet in the form protocol://server domain name/pathname (Protocols are, for instance, HTTP or FTP).

URN
Universal Resource Names remain globally unique and persistent even when the resource ceases to exist or becomes unavailable. A *URN* differs from a URL in that its primary purpose is persistent labelling of a resource with an identifier. Mapping other namespaces on *URNs* is usually straightforward.

W3C
W3C stands for World Wide Web Consortium, which is an industry consortium promoting standards for the evolution of the Web and interoperability between WWW products by providing specifications and reference software. Although *W3C* is funded by industrial members, it is vendor-neutral, and its products are freely available.

Well-formed
Well-formed is a term used to describe an XML document that meets the basic syntax requirements of XML. Note that a well-formed document may not be a valid document according to its schema or DTD.

Working Draft
A *Working Draft* is a W3C publication representing a work in progress and containing a commitment by the W3C to continue the work. A *working draft* does not (yet) imply consensus by a group or the W3C.

XML
The *eXtensible Markup Language* is an utterly simple dialect of SGML. In contrast to SGML documents, *XML* documents may exist without having their schema described in a DTD. *XML* documents consist (mainly) of text and tags, and the tags imply a tree structure upon the document. Is the *XML* document syntactically properly structured, for instance, the tags do correctly nest, the document is said to be 'well-formed' (see [BPSM00 – 2.1 Well-Formed XML Documents] for the other constraints an XML document has to conform to in order to be well-formed). Is there, in addition, a DTD to which the document conforms, it is called 'valid'.

XML declaration

The *XML declaration* is a component at the beginning of an XML document where, for instance, in addition to the version, the character set can be specified:
<?xml version="1.0" encoding="ISO-8859-1"?>.

XML document

An *XML document* consists of the set of nodes and edges in the sub-tree descended from a document node.

XML Infoset (XML Information Set)

XML Infoset is an abstract data set describing the information available from an XML document. For many applications, this way of looking at an XML document is more useful than having to analyse and interpret XML syntax. DOM describes an API through which the information in an *XML Infoset* (the information available from a specific XML document) can be accessed from different programming languages.

XML parser

An *XML parser* is a processor that reads an XML document, determines the structure and properties of the data and interprets them. It breaks the data up into parts and provides them to other components. If the parser does not only check if the XML document is well-formed but also validates the document against an XML DTD, the parser is said to be a 'validating' parser.

XPath

XML Path Language is a language for addressing parts of an XML document, designed to be used by both XSLT and XPointer. The language mainly consists of location paths and expressions. A location path is, for instance, child::country[position=(1)], which selects the first country child of the current context node. Expressions are the usual expressions, for instance, Boolean, numbers, etc. and node sets.

XPointer

XPointer is part of the W3C's XLink standard, specifies how to declare addresses within XLink expressions. *XPointer* specifies the part of a URL behind the '#' that references parts of an XML document, for instance, the fragment identifier. *XPointer* is based on the W3C's XPath Recommendation.

XSL

The *Extensible Stylesheet Language* specifies the styling of an XML document by using XSLT to describe how the document is transformed into another XML document that uses the formatting vocabulary, XSL-FO.

XSLT

XSL Transformations are a language for transforming XML documents into other XML documents. *XSLT* is designed for use as part of XSL.

Appendices

A1 The ACID Properties

ACID stands for:

Atomicity:
All operations of a transaction are either executed to their successful completion (in the case of a commit), or none of them is executed at all (in the case of an abort). In the latter case, all previous changes by the transaction are undone (rollback).

Consistency:
A transaction transforms the database from one consistent state into another consistent state whereby consistency is defined by the semantic constraints of the database – *this includes in particular the required consistency of indices.* Inconsistent states are only allowed as intermediate states while a transaction is ongoing.

Isolation:
Even if many transactions access the same data concurrently, each transaction runs in isolation from concurrent transactions; for instance, a transaction does not see intermediate states of concurrent transactions.

Durability:
Once a transaction has been committed, all of its changes have been written to stable storage.

A2 Semistructured Data

According to Abiteboul [Abi97], these are the most significant aspects of semistructured data:

- The structure is irregular
- The structure is implicit
- The structure is partial
- The structure is less constraining (than, for instance, in the relational data model)
- The schema is derived from the data
- The schema is very large
- The schema is possibly ignored
- The schema is rapidly evolving
- The distinction between the schema and the data is blurred

Bibliography

Note: all URLs have been checked for validity on 01/12/2004

[Abi97]   Serge Abiteboul: *Querying Semi-Structured Data.* In: Proceedings of the Inter-
            national Conference on Database Theory. 1997.

[Bal98]   Helmut Balzert: *Lehrbuch der Software-Technik II: Software-Management,*
            Software-Qualitätssicherung, Unternehmensmodellierung,
            Spektrum Akademischer Verlag, Heidelberg – Berlin, 1998

[BCF+03]   Scott Boag, Don Chamberlin, Mary F. Fernández, Daniela Florescu, Jonathan
            Robie, and Jérôme Siméon: *XQuery 1.0: An XML Query Language.* W3C
            Working Draft, August 2003.
            http://www.w3.org/TR/2003/WD-xquery-20030822/

[BHG87]   Philip A. Bernstein, Vassos Hadzilacos, and Nathan Goodman: *Concurrency*
            Control and Recovery in Database Systems. Addison-Wesley, 1987.

[BHL99]   Tim Bray, Dave Hollander, and Andrew Layman: *Namespaces in XML*
            W3C Recommendation, January 1999.
            http://www.w3.org/TR/1999/REC-xml-names-19990114

[BPSM00]   Tim Bray, Jean Paoli, C. M. Sperberg-McQueen, and Eve Maler:
            Extensible Markup Language (XML) 1.0 (Second Edition)
            W3C Recommendation, October 2000.
            http://www.w3.org/TR/2000/REC-xml-20001006

[CD99]   James Clark and Steve DeRose: *XML Path Language (XPath) Version 1.0*
            W3C Recommendation, November1999.
            http://www.w3.org/TR/1999/REC-xpath-19991116

[CFL+02]   Don Chamberlin, Dana Florescu, Patrick Lehti, Jim Melton, Jonathan Robie,
            Michael Rys, and Jérôme Siméon: *Updates for XQuery*
            W3C Working Draft, 15 October 2002 (not publicly available, only members!).
            http://www.w3.org/TR/2002/WD-xupdate-20021015/

[CFMR03]   Don Chamberlin, Peter Fankhauser, Massimo Marchiori, and Jonathan Robie:
            XML Query (XQuery) Requirements W3C Working Draft, November 2003.
            http://www.w3.org/TR/2003/WD-xquery-requirements-20031112

[Clo04]   Cenqua Pty Ltd.: *Clover User Manual - Version 1.3.* 2004
            http://www.cenqua.com/clover/doc/clover-manual.pdf

[CRZ03]   Akmal B. Chaudri, Awais Rashid, Roberto Zicari (Eds.): *XML Data*
            Management: Native XML and XML-Enabled Database Systems. Addison
            Wesley Professional, March, 2003.

[CSF+01]   Brian F. Cooper, Neal Sample, Michael J. Franklin, Gísli R. Hjaltason, and
            Moshe Shadmon: *A Fast Index for Semistructured Data.* In: Proceedings of
            the 27th International Conference on Very Large Data Bases (VLDB 2001),
            Rome, Italy, 2001, pages 341-350. Morgan Kaufmann.
            http://www.vldb.org/conf/2001/P341.pdf

[CT01]   John Cowan and Richard Tobin: *XML Information Set*
             W3C Recommendation, October 2001.
             http://www.w3.org/TR/2001/REC-xml-infoset-20011024

[DBLP]   Michael Ley (caretaker): *DBLP Computer Science Bibliography*
             http://www.informatik.uni-trier.de/~ley/db/

[Die82]   Paul F. Dietz: *Maintaining order in a linked list.* In: *Proceedings of the Four-
             teenth Annual ACM Symposium on Theory of Computing,*
             pages 122–127, San Francisco, California, May 1982.

[Fal01]   David C. Fallside: *XML Schema Part 0: Primer*
             W3C Recommendation, October 2004.
             http://www.w3.org/TR/2004/REC-xmlschema-0-20041028/

[FMM+01]   Mary Fernández, Ashok Malhotra, Jonathan Marsh (XSL WG), Marton Nagy,
             and Norman Walsh: *XQuery 1.0 and XPath 2.0 Data Model*
             W3C Working Draft, May 2003.
             http://www.w3.org/TR/2003/WD-xpath-datamodel-20030502/

[Gru02]   Torsten Grust: *Accelerating XPath location steps.* In: Proceedings of the 2002
             ACM SIGMOD International Conference on Management of Data, Madison,
             Wisconsin, USA, 2002, pages 109-120. ACM, 2002.

[GW97]   Roy Goldman and Jennifer Widom: *DataGuides: Enabling Query Formulation
             and Optimization in Semistructured Databases.* In: Proceedings of the 23rd In-
             ternational Conference on Very Large Data Bases (VLDB 1997), Athens,
             Greece, 1997, pages 436-445. Morgan Kaufmann, 1997.
             http://citeseer.nj.nec.com/126680.html

[GW99]   Roy Goldman and Jennifer Widom: *Approximate DataGuides.* In Proceedings
             of the Workshop on Query Processing for Semistructured Data and Non-Stan-
             dard Data Formats, Jerusalem, Israel, January 1999.
             http://citeseer.nj.nec.com/goldman99approximate.html

[HMF99]   Gerald Huck, Ingo Macherius, and Peter Fankhauser: *PDOM: Lightweight
             Persistency Support for the Document Object Model.* In: Proceedings of the
             OOPSLA Workshop on Java and Databases: Persistence Options, 1999.
             http://www.ipsi.fraunhofer.de/oasys/reports/ftp/pdf/P1999-27.pdf

[HMF01]   Gerald Huck, Ingo Macherius, and Peter Fankhauser: *PDOM: Lightweight
             Persistency Support.* In: *Succeeding with Object Databases*, pages 107-118.
             John Wiley, 2001.

[HHW+00]   Arnaud Le Hors, Philippe Le Hégaret, Lauren Wood, Gavin Nicol, Jonathan
             Robie, Mike Champion, and Steve Byrne:
             Document Object Model (DOM) Level 2 Core Specification.
             W3C Recommendation, November 2000.
             http://www.w3.org/TR/2000/REC-DOM-Level-2-Core-20001113

[HHW+03]   Arnaud Le Hors, Philippe Le Hégaret, Lauren Wood, Gavin Nicol, Jonathan
             Robie, Mike Champion, and Steve Byrne:
             Document Object Model (DOM) Level 3 Core Specification.
             W3C Recommendation, April 2004.
             http://www.w3.org/TR/2004/REC-DOM-Level-3-Core-20040407

[Info03]   Infonyte GmbH: *Infonyte DB - User Manual and Programmers Guide,*
             Version 3.1.0   (comes with the evaluation version of Infonyte DB)
             http://www.infonyte.com/en/down_product.jsp

[KYU01]   Dao Dinh Kha, Masatoshi Yoshikawa, and Shunsuke Uemura: *An XML In-*
             dexing Structure with Relative Region Coordinate. In: Proceedings of the 17th
             International Conference on Data Engineering (ICDE 2001), Heidelberg, Ger-
             many, 2001, pages 313-320. IEEE Computer Society, 2001.
             http://citeseer.nj.nec.com/kha01xml.html

[Leh01]   Patrick Lehti: *Design and Implementation of a Data Manipulation Processor for*
             an XML Query Language. Diplomarbeit, August 2001.
             http://www.lehti.de/beruf/diplomarbeit.pdf

[Lig90]   Liggesmeyer, Peter: *Modultest und Modulverifikation.*
             BI-Wissenschaftsverlag, Mannheim/Wien/Zürich, 1990

[LM00]   Andreas Laux and Lars Martin: *XUpdate - XML Update Language.*
             September 2000.
             http://xmldb-org.sourceforge.net/xupdate/xupdate-wd.html

[LM01]   Quanzhong Li and Bongki Moon: *Indexing and Querying XML Data for Regu-*
             lar Path Expressions. In: Proceedings of the 27th International Conference on
             Very Large Data Bases (VLDB 2001), Rome, Italy, 2001, pages 361-370.
             Morgan Kaufmann, 2001.
             http://citeseer.nj.nec.com/li01indexing.html

[Lov68]   Julie Beth Lovins: *Development of a stemming algorithm.* In: Mechanical
             translation and computational linguistics 11, pages 1-2, 22-31, 1968.

[Mar00]   Lars Martin: *XML Update Language Requirements.* November 2000.
             http://xmldb-org.sourceforge.net/xupdate/xupdate-req.html

[Mei02]   Wolfgang M. Meier: *eXist: An Open Source Native XML Database.* In: Web,
             Web-Services, and Database Systems. NODe 2002 Web- and Database-
             Related Workshops, Erfurt, Germany, October 2002. Springer LNCS Series
             2593

[Mei04]   Wolfgang M. Meier: *eXist Native XML Database.*
             http://exist.sourceforge.net/index.html

[Mye79]   Glenford J. Myers: *The Art of Software Testing.*
             John Wiley & Sons. New York, 1979.

[Por80]   Martin F. Porter: *An algorithm for suffix stripping.* In: Program, Volume 14 (No.
             3), pages 130-137, July 1980.

[RFC2119]   Scott Bradner: *Key words for use in RFCs to Indicate Requirement Levels.*
             March 1997.
             http://www.ietf.org/rfc/rfc2119.txt

[TIHW01]   Igor Tatarinov, Zachary G. Ives, Alon Y. Halevy, and Daniel S. Weld:
            Updating XML. In: Proceedings of the 2001 ACM SIGMOD International Con-
            ference on Management of data, Santa Barbara, California USA, 2001,
            pages 413-424.
            http://www.cs.washington.edu/homes/zives/research/updatingXML.pdf

[XIND04]   The Apache Group: *Xindice Native XML Database.*
            http://xml.apache.org/xindice